Oliver Optic

Brake up: The young peacemakers

Oliver Optic

Brake up: The young peacemakers

ISBN/EAN: 9783337223311

Printed in Europe, USA, Canada, Australia, Japan

Cover: Foto ©ninafisch / pixelio.de

More available books at **www.hansebooks.com**

THE LAKE SHORE SERIES.

BRAKE UP;

OR,

THE YOUNG PEACEMAKERS.

BY

OLIVER OPTIC,

AUTHOR OF "YOUNG AMERICA ABROAD," "THE ARMY AND NAVY STORIES," "THE WOODVILLE STORIES," "THE BOAT-CLUB STORIES," "THE STARRY FLAG STORIES," ETC.

BOSTON:
LEE AND SHEPARD, PUBLISHERS.
NEW YORK:
LEE, SHEPARD AND DILLINGHAM.
1873.

TO

MY YOUNG FRIEND

ELLIOT WILLIAM SAYWARD

𝕿𝖍𝖎𝖘 𝕭𝖔𝖔𝖐

IS AFFECTIONATELY DEDICATED.

THE LAKE SHORE SERIES.

1. *THROUGH BY DAYLIGHT;* or, The Young Engineer of the Lake Shore Railroad.

2. *LIGHTNING EXPRESS;* or, The Rival Academies.

3. *ON TIME;* or, The Young Captain of the Ucayga Steamer.

4. *SWITCH OFF;* or, The War of the Students.

5. *BRAKE UP;* or, The Young Peacemakers.

6. *BEAR AND FORBEAR;* or, The Young Skipper of Lake Ucayga.

PREFACE.

"BRAKE UP" is the fifth of THE LAKE SHORE SERIES, and was one of the serials which appeared in Oliver Optic's Magazine. Although the volume contains an independent story, the same characters that appeared in preceding issues of the series are introduced. While Captain Wolf Penniman still remains true to his high standard of duty, Nick Von Wolter is presented to the reader in strong contrast with the hero. The latter, ambitious to put himself forward in the world, makes the oft-repeated mistake of those who follow any other guide than that of religious principle. The result to the evil-doer is but the reflection of the world's experience; and though all who seek and follow the True Light may not realize the same worldly success that crowned the life of Wolf, they are absolutely sure to attain that peace of mind which alone is happiness here and hereafter.

The railroad phrase "BRAKE UP" is not used in its technical sense, but figuratively indicates how the wrong-doer should proceed when he becomes conscious of his error; and the author hopes his young friends, as well as those of mature years, will follow the example of the magnate of Centreport when they find themselves on the "wrong track."

HARRISON SQUARE, BOSTON,
January 26, 1870.

CONTENTS.

CHAPTER I.
PAGE
COLONEL WIMPLETON WON'T HAVE IT. 11

CHAPTER II.
BRAKE UP! 20

CHAPTER III.
MR. NICHOLAS VAN WOLTER. 31

CHAPTER IV.
A GLORIOUS OPPORTUNITY. 41

CHAPTER V.
ROMANCE AND REALITY. 52

CHAPTER VI.
A DISCOMFITED ASPIRANT. 63

CHAPTER VII.
COLONEL WIMPLETON DROPS THE REINS. 74

CHAPTER VIII.
SECRETS FOR TWO. 84

CONTENTS.

CHAPTER IX.
The Tipsy Magnate. 96

CHAPTER X.
Tom Walton expresses his Opinion. 106

CHAPTER XI.
A Generous Tippler. 117

CHAPTER XII.
Another Calamity. 128

CHAPTER XIII.
After the Accident. 139

CHAPTER XIV.
"The Occurrences of Yesterday." 150

CHAPTER XV.
A Tempting Offer. 162

CHAPTER XVI.
The Ucayga in Trouble. 173

CHAPTER XVII.
An Act of Courtesy. 185

CHAPTER XVIII.
The Mystery of the Check. 196

CHAPTER XIX.
Colonel Wimpleton humiliated. 208

CHAPTER XX.
A Night Trip to Hitaca. 220

CHAPTER XXI.
What happened in the Road. 232

CHAPTER XXII.
Seven per cent. Bonds. 244

CHAPTER XXIII.
The Committee of Conference. 256

CHAPTER XXIV.
The Magnates join Hands. 268

CHAPTER XXV.
More seven per cent. Bonds. 280

CHAPTER XXVI.
In Honor of the Reconciliation. 292

BRAKE UP;

OR,

THE YOUNG PEACEMAKERS.

CHAPTER I.

COLONEL WIMPLETON WON'T HAVE IT.

"I WON'T have it, Wolf Penniman! No, I won't have it!" said and repeated Colonel Wimpleton, as, with an uncertain step, he shuffled up to the door of my state-room, on board of the Ucayga.

The magnate of Centreport was more than usually intoxicated. For two or three years he had kept himself well filled with rum. His face had grown red, and toddy-blossoms had gathered upon his aquiline nose, but he seldom manifested any of the ordinary symptoms of drunkenness. It was not often that he reeled, or became incoherent in his speech, as on the present occasion. If he was ever overcome by his besetting vice, it was not in public. I had certainly never before seen him in the condition in which he presented himself at the door of my state-room.

I was aware that the habit of drinking was gaining upon him. I had frequently seen him when he was affected by the liquor he had taken. I had known him to fall asleep in company when the conversation flagged, and I had often noticed the stupor of inebriation. He took less interest in the steamer, and in other business enterprises in which he was engaged, than formerly. Under the influence of his drams, when excited, he was even more violent than when he was sober. For years he had been the deadly enemy of Major Toppleton, the rich man of Middleport, on the opposite side of the lake. His intemperance did not moderate his hatred, though it deprived him of the energy to prosecute malicious schemes against his rival.

Three years before, Major Toppleton had completed the Lake Shore Railroad, intended in the beginning rather as a plaything for the students of the Toppleton Institute, and as a means of giving the young men a knowledge of railroad business, though the idea had enlarged on his hands, and the line had become a regular thoroughfare of travel. A violent competition had sprung up between the two sides of the lake. The projector of the railroad had purchased the old line of steamers, and ran them only to Middleport, thus compelling the people of the large and thriving town of Centreport to do all their business through the rival place on the other side of the lake. This was more than the choleric temper of Colonel Wimpleton could endure, and he immediately built the large, swift, and beautiful steamer Ucayga, to run between Centreport and the lower end of the lake, thus giving the town direct communication with the great business centres of the nation.

For a time the Lake Shore line had the advantage, and obtained nearly all the through business; but the new steamer, of which I had the honor to be captain, by making one through trip a day to Hitaca, at the upper extremity of the lake, beating the railroad line by three quarters of an hour, and affording better accommodation, without change from boat to cars and from cars to boat, turned the current of travel, and

Centreport obtained a complete and decided victory over Middleport. Of course Major Toppleton was sorely vexed at the triumph of his great rival. He had vainly sought the means of recovering his lost prestige. The best time he could make was four hours and a quarter, while the steamer line accomplished the distance in three and a half. He could regain the ground he had lost only by building a steamer like the Ucayga, or extending his railroad through a wild region for twenty-five miles, to the head of the lake. Either of these expedients involved a very large outlay of money, which he was not willing to make. But he continued to talk of doing something, and there was no end to the agitation of the subject.

I had certain very decided views of my own, and earnestly hoped that the major would adopt neither of his expensive expedients. All Middleport and all Centreport had been at war with each other for years. Not only the major and the colonel, but their two sons, and the two academies under their patronage, had hated and fought each other; but now all had been reconciled except the two magnates, though the business rivalry between the two places was not abated. But it seemed to me that, after the two sons had become good friends and the two Institutes had fraternized, the two magnates hated each other more bitterly than ever. I could not help fearing that a new steamer, or an extension of the railroad, would increase the malignant rivalry; and, acting through Tommy Toppleton, the major's son, and Waddie Wimpleton, the colonel's son, I had done what I could to keep the two lines as they were at the opening of my present story.

Major Toppleton had proposed to me, and I had suggested to Colonel Wimpleton, the plan of uniting the two lines; but the magnate of Centreport had indignantly and scornfully repudiated the proposition. He would have nothing to do with the Toppletons. Such a union would be a benefit to the travelling public, while it would afford a remunerative business to each line. It would reduce the time from Hitaca to Ucayga three quarters of an hour, and make an end of all the ill feeling engendered by the competition. The one purpose of my existence, at this time, was to accomplish this union. I hoped and prayed for some happy circumstance that would reconcile the great men. I was even daring enough to attempt to contrive a plan by which this blessed result might be attained; but I had not been able to devise any expedient which appeared hopeful enough to be attempted.

Colonel Wimpleton was more than usually intoxicated when he presented himself at the door of my state-room. As he spoke he staggered into the apartment, and dropped heavily into a chair. It was mortifying and disgusting even to me to see him in this condition; but how much more so to his family! I pitied his wife, I pitied Waddie, and I pitied Minnie Wimpleton, the oldest daughter of the magnate; indeed, I pitied all who were connected with him; for if he was a terrible man when sober, he was vastly more terrible when intoxicated. Though he had occasionally found fault with me since I had been in charge of the steamer, he never indulged in anything which could be called abuse. On the other hand, if anybody could be said to have any influence over him, I had a very little. It was by my plans, and through my direct agency, that the steamer had won the victory over the rival line. I had always treated him with respect, and even with "distinguished consideration," but at the same time I maintained my independence. The colonel knew that the moment he cast me off, the major was ready to take me up, and restore me to my old position on the railroad. Perhaps it is not exactly modest for me to state these things, but it would be mere affectation for me to ignore them.

"I won't have it!" repeated Colonel Wimpleton, with greater emphasis, as he dropped into the chair in my state-room.

"What, sir?" I inquired.

"I say I won't have it," he replied, fixing a kind of vacant stare upon the floor.

I concluded that what he would not have related to the steamer, and I was prepared to receive the rebuke he had apparently come to administer. I could think of nothing I had done to deserve censure. The Ucayga had made all her trips with clock-work regularity. We had been "on time;" and except when the days were too short, we had put her "through by daylight." The pleasure season was just opening, and we were carrying crowds of passengers. Certainly everything seemed to be lovely, and I was not conscious of deserving a rebuke. But in my relations with the colonel I often received what I did not deserve. I was tolerably intimate in the family of Major Toppleton. Tommy, now thoroughly reformed, was one of my best friends. He was grateful to me because I had assisted in saving him from the wrath of Jed Trotwood, and as he still had a great influence over his father, he always insured me a welcome at the Toppleton mansion.

Grace Toppleton was very kindly disposed towards me; and being eighteen now, I am willing to confess that I believed her to be the prettiest and the dearest girl in the whole world. I had become very particular in regard to my dress, and my mother often declared that she was afraid I should yet be a dandy, I was so particular to wear good clothes, and to have my neck-tie nicely adjusted. But, then, I was the commander of the Ucayga, and it was a part of my duty to make myself agreeable to the passengers, including many elegant and accomplished ladies. Yet I could not conceal from myself the truth that I cared more for the opinion of Grace than of all others. For her I wore the good clothes; for her I was particular about my neck-tie; and for her I brushed my hair till every individual lock had found its most graceful position. By continued perseverance in shaving my upper lip, I had coaxed a tolerable mustache into being, which, I fondly believed, not only overcame the juvenility of my appearance, but added a manly feature to my face.

I was very much interested in Grace, as I had been from the first moment I saw her. Indeed, this interest had grown upon me in a manner which I need not stop to explain. I acknowledged to myself that I had "intentions" in regard to her, though I could not help feeling that they were very presumptuous in me, who had neither a great name nor a great family to boast of. I had never said anything to Grace about these intentions, but I flattered myself that she was not wholly indifferent towards me. Her father did not seem to notice my attentions, but I was afraid he would. As this was the thought always nearest to my heart, it occurred to me, as the tipsy colonel sat looking at the floor in my state-room, that my devotion to Grace was what he would not have.

CHAPTER II.

BRAKE UP!

I LOOKED at Colonel Wimpleton, as he sat gazing, with a stupid stare, upon the floor of the state-room. I began to feel some trepidation lest my relations with the family of Major Toppleton were to be criticised and censured. But true to the instincts of all young men in my situation, I was ready to die rather than yield the breadth of a hair in my devotion to Grace. The magnates might quarrel as much as suited their imperial pleasure, but I would neither be coaxed nor driven into the feud. I was resolved to be discharged from my pleasant and lucrative position rather than have my agreeable relations with the Toppletons suspended.

"Wolf, I won't have it!" exclaimed the colonel, suddenly, as he stamped his foot upon the floor, after a silence which enabled me to review my previous conduct for months.

"What, sir?" I inquired again.

But the tipsy magnate did not condescend to reply to my question. He contracted the muscles of his face into a maudlin expression of indignation, and continued to brood over the evil which disturbed him.

"You must go with me, Wolf," said he, after another long pause.

"Where, sir?"

"Over to Middleport.— No, I won't have it! I'll put a stop to it!"

"I really don't understand you, Colonel Wimpleton," I pleaded.

"You don't understand it, Wolf? Yes, you do understand it, Wolf. You know all about it."

"What, sir?"

"What, sir!" sneered the colonel, fixing a stare of drunken ire upon me. "You must go with me, Wolf."

"But the boat must start in less than an hour," I added, consulting my watch.

"I don't care for the boat. This thing is of more consequence than the boat, Wolf."

"What thing, sir?"

"Boys musn't be men till they are old enough to

be men, Wolf," protested the great man. "Come with me."

He rose with some difficulty from the chair, and tottered towards the door.

"Where am I to go, sir?" I asked.

"Over to the other side of the lake."

"But the boat—"

"Don't say any more to me about the boat, Wolf. Van Wolter can run the boat as well as you can. Come along with me."

"Very well, sir; I will tell Mr. Van Wolter that I shall not go down the lake with him."

When I had seen the mate, I returned to my stateroom, where the colonel had again seated himself. I kept a tumbler and a pitcher of ice water in the room, and as I went to take a drink, I found the glass smelled strongly of liquor. The magnate had a bottle in his pocket, and had taken another dram. I did not like to go with him while he was in his present condition, and evidently growing worse, but I could not refuse without creating a tempest.

"Courting!" ejaculated the colonel, as I put on my cap. "I won't have it."

"I don't understand you, sir," I replied, startled by the suggestive word he had used.

"You'll understand it very soon, Wolf, for I won't have it. Come with me."

What could the great man mean? Did he apply that word to my relations with Grace Toppleton? I was not willing to have them called by so vulgar a term. He rose from the chair, and bolted out of the state-room, for he could not now maintain a steady gait. I followed him to the gangway, where the boat I had ordered was waiting for us. Van Wolter winked at me as I passed him, and seemed to regard the drunkenness of the magnate as a good joke, instead of the most serious thing in the world. With the assistance of the mate and myself, the colonel succeeded in depositing himself in the boat without falling into the lake, and the men landed us at Middleport.

Bracing up his nerves to their utmost tension, the great man walked up the wharf to the railroad station, whence he dropped into a chair, overcome by his exertions to act like a sober man. The last dram imbibed had not yet produced its full effect, and I hoped, in the stupor of intoxication, he would forget his mission, whatever it was. People looked at him, smiled, winked, and sneered, as he sat in the waiting-room, and it was very disagreeable to me to be obliged to be his companion. There is no knowing what a tipsy man may do, and I was fearful that he would place me in a still more embarrassing position. The vulgar expression he had used — "courting" — indicated that there was a lady in the affair. I suspected that he meant to proceed to the house of Major Toppleton; but I was determined not to go there with him, for such a step would imply that he intended to meddle with my affair.

"No, I won't have it, Wolf! Now go and see where they have gone," said the colonel, after he had sat a few moments.

"See where who have gone, sir?" I inquired.

"Why, Tom Toppleton and Waddie."

"I know where they have gone."

"Where?" he demanded, jerking up his head suddenly.

"Down to the Horse Shoe, sir."

"I suppose you know all about it."

"They have gone to select a camp for the regiment — that's all."

"No, sir! That's not all, Wolf! You know very well that's not all."

"At least, that's all I know about it," I pleaded.

"Now, where's Grace Toppleton? That's what I want to know," said he, savagely.

"I don't know where she is," I replied, not pleased to have her name connected with the matter, whatever it might prove to be.

"You go and find out where she is — that's what I want you to do. Don't talk to me! I tell you I won't have it."

"I will ascertain where she is," I replied, not unwilling to call at the house of the major, where I might see her.

"Go, and don't stop long."

I did go, and I did not stop long. Grace was not at home. She had gone to the Horse Shoe in the same boat with Tommy, where he was to meet Waddie. I reported this intelligence to the colonel.

"That is just what I supposed!" exclaimed he, springing to his feet. "I won't have it. Get two tickets, Wolf, and take me to the Horse Shoe."

"I will, sir."

"Courting!" snuffed the colonel.

"Who, sir?"

"In love."

"Who, sir?"

"I won't have it! No, I won't."

By this time I began to believe that I was not the object of his suspicion; but I was very anxious to know who was implicated in this grave charge of "courting," or of being in love. I knew that Nick Van Wolter, the mate's son, had gone down to the Horse Shoe with Waddie, in the Raven; and now it appeared that Tommy and Grace had also gone. My present information assured me that Grace was the only young lady of the party, and if any "courting" was meditated, it was plain to me, from the nature of the circumstances, that she must be one of the parties.

I confess that I began to feel very uneasy when the possibility of the occasion dawned upon me. Grace, so far as I knew, was the only lady in the party. If any one was in love with her, who could it be? Certainly it was not Tommy; and it was almost as certain that it could not be Nick Van Wolter, though the latter was a very conceited young man, with assurance enough to fall in love with one so much his superior as Grace. But if it was Nick, why should the colonel trouble himself about the matter? I was satisfied that it could not be Nick. Then it must be Waddie.

My blood seemed to grow cold in my veins as the only reasonable explanation of the problem was forced upon my mind. Such an event would inflame the magnate of Centreport to wrath, for he could conceive of no more terrible calamity than an alliance by marriage between the rival families. I was shocked and confounded. Yet I was reasonable enough to believe that it was the most natural thing in the world for Waddie to fall in love with Grace. She was beautiful and winning beyond any words of mine to express. He was socially her equal, which I was not. Distressed as I was, I could offer no objection to the idea.

I procured two tickets for Grass Springs, and assisted the colonel into the rear car. He still persisted that he would not "have it," talked wild, foolish, and angry, by turns, till the stupor of his last dram overcame him, and he dropped asleep, much to my satisfaction, for I was disgusted with his speech. Besides,

I did not feel like talking with any one. I had experienced a terrible blow. I had lost Grace Toppleton. I had mistaken her kindness to me for a more tender sentiment, and I felt like lying down on the bottom of the lake in deep water, or emigrating to some distant and unknown region.

The cars stopped a moment at Spangleport. Major Toppleton had built a bridge over the outlet of the lake, so that the train ran into Ucayga, thus gaining time enough to allow the stops at the two towns on the route. The dummy also made two trips a day to Grass Springs, so that the people along the line were better accommodated than ever before. About half way between Spangleport and the Springs, the engineer whistled furiously, and the train began to brake up rather sharply.

"What's the matter, Wolf?" said the colonel, awaking with a start.

"I don't know, sir; perhaps a cow is on the track."

"Go ahead and see," said he, thrusting his hand into his breast pocket, where he must have kept his bottle.

I obeyed him, and as I opened the forward door, I

saw him drinking from his flask. I had walked through three cars, when the train stopped. As I had supposed, an obstinate cow had placed herself on the track, and not having the fear of locomotives before her, refused to budge till the fireman drove her off by pelting her with coal. The train started again, and I did not hurry back to the colonel; but when I reached the rear of the last car, he was not there. I was alarmed, and immediately looked through the train for him. I could not find him. The passengers had not observed him. I was afraid he had fallen off, and I hastened to find the conductor.

He was in the forward car. I stated the case to him, and begged him to run back a little way. After many objections he consented, and gave the order. A brakeman was sent to the rear platform, but the conductor detained me to tell me the consequences that might follow the delay. I promised to help him out on some other occasion when he was behind time, by inducing the conductors on the great line to wait for him. I hastened back to the rear platform, but before I could reach it, I heard the whistle to brake up. On reaching the end of the car, I saw a sight which froze my blood. Colonel Wimpleton lay on the track between the rails, apparently unable to save himself.

The brakeman had pulled the connecting line, and was jamming down the brake with all his might; but it was still a problem whether the train could be stopped in season to avoid running over him. I rushed to the assistance of the man, and the brake creaked under our united efforts. Fortunately the signal from the engine had been prompt, and the train was stopped, but only a few feet from the tipsy magnate, who shook his fist at the car as it came near.

"Did ye mean to run over me?" said he; and it was evident that his last dram had nearly finished him.

[We intended to let Wolf tell his own story, but we are obliged to take the pen out of his hand, for a time, to relate certain incidents of which he was not a witness. Nicholas Van Wolter is no scholar; and if he were, we could not trust him to narrate the matter of the succeeding chapters, for we fear he would suppress the truth, and introduce too much of his own personal vanity.]

CHAPTER III.

MR. NICHOLAS VAN WOLTER.

MR. NICK VAN WOLTER, a young gentleman of eighteen, and the oldest son of the mate of the Ucayga, was dressing himself with extraordinary care on the morning preceding the incidents of the last chapter. He was very little like his father, who was a plain, honest, straightforward man, and very much like his mother, who was a vain, aspiring, ambitious woman. The mate was willing to do his duty faithfully and patiently, and let the future take care of itself, though he was not without a reasonable ambition to distinguish himself, and make his fortune. His wife thought the world, and particularly Colonel Wimpleton, had wronged and defrauded her husband out of money and position. She had high hopes of Nick, for he was of an aspiring nature, and did not believe that he had yet found his true sphere.

Nick had brushed his hair with remarkable precision; he had carefully laid each individual hair of his downy mustache; and he was now engaged in the difficult and trying operation of tying his cravat. He had donned his Sunday clothes, though it was Monday, and though he was going in the Raven, which was the name of Waddie Wimpleton's new sail-boat. The fact that Miss Minnie Wimpleton was to be one of the party may explain the reason of all the extra pains the young man bestowed upon himself. Miss Wimpleton was certainly a very beautiful girl, though this need not have made any difference with Nick, who had only been invited to help work the Raven, for Waddie had a lame arm, wrenched at the shoulder in playing base ball.

It would be difficult to describe the precise social or business position of Nick Van Wolter. He had worked on the steamer as a deck hand, and as a waiter in the cabin; but he had become disgusted with both of these places. They were beneath his dignity, and below his sphere. He had obtained a place in a store in Centreport, where his father's family resided; but sweeping out, working in the cellars, and carrying bundles were so far beneath his aspirations that he had also abandoned the store. He now appeared to be "waiting for something to turn up." He wanted to be the clerk of the Ucayga, as a stepping-stone to a higher place; but the present incumbent obstinately persisted in retaining the situation. He was devoted, mind, heart, and soul, to Waddie Wimpleton, through whom he expected finally to accomplish his purpose. He was willing to "toady" to the great man's son, to bow down before him, and cling to the skirts of his garments. When Waddie, therefore, in his partially disabled condition, needed assistance in the boat, Nick was available for the service, and had gladly accepted the invitation.

Nick labored heavily at the neck-tie, and his ambitious mother stood in the middle of the floor, watching with interest the effect produced by various experiments. Bow knots, square knots, and sailor's knots were successively tried and successively discarded, until it was evident that the cravat would be worn out before it could be adjusted. But at last Mrs. Van Wolter interfered, and insisted that a simple crossing of the ends of the tie, fastened by a large breast-pin, which was borrowed from the mate's wardrobe, gave the most stunning effect. She was satisfied, and Nick could devise nothing better, though he was not wholly pleased.

"Now, let me put this moss-rose on the lapel of your coat," said the devoted mother. "If Miss Wimpleton thinks it is a pretty one, or makes any remark about it, be sure you make her a present of it."

"I don't think she cares anything about me," replied Nick, as he glanced at the looking-glass to observe the effect of the rose.

"Well, I don't suppose she does; but you must make her care for you. If you have any wit at all, you can make yourself useful and agreeable. Why, look at Wolf Penniman. They do say that he and Grace Toppleton are good friends, at the very least. Wolf is smart; he knows what he is about."

"So do I know what I am about," retorted Nick, repelling what appeared to him to be an insinuation that he did *not* know what he was about. "If there is any such thing as getting on the right side of Minnie Wimpleton, you will find me there."

"I hope so. You ought to be as high up in the

world as Wolf Penniman. You are a better looking fellow," added the fond mother, gazing with admiration at the form and features of her son. "If you are not as smart as he, it is because you have never put yourself forward, and it is high time for you to begin. There's Wolf, captain of the Ucayga, while you can't even be clerk. It's a shame. I know your father ought to be captain of that steamer, for he has really run the boat, while Wolf has had all the credit of it. But I can't get your father to do anything about it."

"Father is his own master," said Nick, with something like malice in his tones.

"I know he is. If he would hear to me, he would be captain of the steamer, and you would be clerk. Only to think of it! Your father, who has been a steamboat man all the days of his life, acting as mate to a boy, a mere snipper-snapper, who don't know any more about managing a steamboat than I do! It's a shame! I can't bear to think of it!"

"Don't, then."

"Well, if your father won't do anything for the family, you must, Nicholas. Waddie is your best friend; and, if you can only make an impression upon

Miss Minnie, your fortune will be made, for I don't believe the colonel will live a great many years. He is soaked in rum all the time."

"If I only get the chance, mother, I shall show Minnie who and what I am. She is very gentle and kind to me, and all I want is an opportunity to lay myself out before her."

"If you don't find the chance, make it, Nicholas — make it."

Nick was thoughtful at this suggestion. It seemed to be a new idea to him. He had devoted no inconsiderable portion of his valuable time to the reading of exciting romances, and he was confident that if he could obtain the opportunity to save Miss Minnie from a watery grave, rescue her from a burning house, or stay the mad flight of her runaway horse, just as she was about to be dashed to pieces over a yawning precipice, doing the noble deed at the imminent peril of his own life, the prize would be won. The proud daughter of a noble house would be filled with admiration and gratitude, and would, of course, fall in love with him, and the third part of Colonel Wimpleton's millions would drop into his lap. The last chapter of the romance would end in the unutterable bliss of the noble hero and the beautiful heroine. This was about the idea Nick had of "a chance to lay himself out before her." He wanted such a chance, and his mother, doubtless without exactly comprehending her son's views, had suggested that he should make the chance. The thought was worthy of consideration.

"Your father is too tame and spiritless to do anything for the family. You must do it for him, Nicholas," added Mrs. Van Wolter.

"I'm willing to do what I can," meekly responded the hopeful son.

"If you do, your father shall be captain of the steamer; you shall be clerk, and in good time the husband of Miss Minnie."

"What do you mean, mother? You don't expect me to make father captain — do you?"

"Well, well; we won't talk about that now," answered the mother, evasively. "We must use circumstances for our own advantage."

Mrs. Van Wolter appeared to be a bold schemer, and even Nick was astonished at the magnitude of her ideas. He was looking for a brilliant future, and to his mind there was no reason why Wolf Penniman should monopolize all the honors and all the emoluments of the high positions. He put on his hat, and left the house. He was rather anxious to know by what means his mother expected to promote the mate to the captaincy, and to make him the clerk of the steamer; but his present business was in relation to Minnie Wimpleton, and he hastened to the pier where the Raven was moored.

Nick was only a tolerable boatman; and he was not conceited in regard to his ability to manage a sail-boat. He was willing to take lessons of Waddie, who had no superior. Indeed, he yielded the palm in everything to the young magnate. He hoisted the mainsail, and put everything in order about the boat. By the time he had finished the preparations for the trip, Waddie and his sister appeared. The young gentleman had his arm in a sling, and the young lady, in the estimation of Nick, was radiant with loveliness.

"Good morning, Mr. Van Wolter," said Minnie, as she arrived at the pier.

There was a twinkle in her eye, and one would have judged there was no little mischief in her composition.

She glanced at the elaborate toilet, and particularly at the huge breast-pin in the cravat of the aspiring Nick. Perhaps she was vain enough to suspect that all this extra preparation had been made for her sake.

"Good morning, Miss Wimpleton," replied Nick, removing his hat with an extensive flourish, probably to afford the wealthy little divinity an opportunity to see how nicely his hair was parted, oiled, and brushed. "May I have the pleasure of assisting you on board the Raven?"

"Will it be a pleasure, Mr. Van Wolter?" said she, mischievously, as she extended her gloved hand to him.

"A very great pleasure indeed, Miss Wimpleton," he replied, as he eagerly took the offered hand, his heart beating like the throes of an earthquake, under the delicious sensations of the moment.

He handed her to a seat in the standing-room, touched his hat, and bowed, as if to thank her for the unexpected honor she had conferred upon him.

"Cast off, and run up the jib, Nick," said Waddie, impatiently. "We are going to have a shower to-day, and we must get up to Grass Springs before it comes on."

"A shower, Waddie?" added Minnie.

"It looks like one."

"I don't want to go if it is to be rainy."

"Only a shower. The cabin will keep you as dry as your own room," answered Waddie. "There is a good breeze, and we shall be down there in a couple of hours."

"It will spoil Nick's new clothes," laughed the sprightly miss.

"Don't you tease the simpleton," whispered Waddie.

"I can't help it. I enjoy it hugely," she replied.

"There goes the Belle," added Waddie, pointing to Wolf's boat, which Tommy Toppleton had chartered for the occasion, as she shot out from the wharf at Middleport. "Now for a race!"

Nick ran up the jib, and, as the Raven took the breeze, he seated himself opposite Miss Minnie, to feast his eyes upon her "matchless loveliness."

CHAPTER IV.

A GLORIOUS OPPORTUNITY.

THE boat-builder at Hitaca had promised Waddie he should have a boat that would beat the Belle, or any other craft of her inches on the lake. He had evidently kept his word, though the respective merits of the two boats had not yet been fairly tested; but, in building for speed, he had not built for safety. The Raven was too narrow for her length, and it was apparent that she was very crank. However, Waddie did not care how crank she was, if she was only fast. He was skilful enough himself to keep her right side up.

Tom Walton was sailing the Belle, and Tommy Toppleton and Grace were passengers. Though the trip to the Horse Shoe was for another purpose, the race between the two boats could not well be avoided. Waddie was anxious to have the point settled, and as Tom Walton, the regular skipper of the Belle, was on board, the race commenced without a challenge, or any other preparations. The Belle waited until the Raven came out from the wharf, and they met in the middle of the lake, where the two parties exchanged salutations.

"I'm afraid we shall have some bad weather," said Tom Walton, as he glanced at the black clouds which were piling up in the south-west.

"We shall get to the Horse Shoe before that shower comes up," replied Waddie, as he put his helm up, and the Raven filled away on her course.

"Let her slide!" shouted Tom Walton, who was not yet quite ready to believe that the new boat could beat the Belle.

"So we are to have a race, Waddie," said his sister, as the Belle shaped her course for the Horse Shoe.

"Yes; and I'm going to beat the Belle all to pieces," answered Waddie, in high excitement, as the two boats, now side by side, began to spin furiously through the water, the spray curling over their bows, as they bent down before the lively breeze.

"But you will drown us all, Waddie!" exclaimed

Minnie, as the Raven careened under a flaw till the gunwale was nearly submerged.

"There is not the least danger while Mr. Wimpleton is at the helm. He is the most skilful boatman on the lake," interposed Nick.

"But I don't like such furious sailing as this," added Minnie, as half a bucket of spray dashed upon the half deck forward of her.

"Don't be alarmed, Minnie," said Waddie, gently. "She is doing beautifully, and we are gaining on the Belle. I wish my arm was not so lame. It bothers me."

"I cannot steer as well as you can, Waddie; but I will do the best I can," added Nick.

"If we were on the other tack I could do it very well; but I don't like to sit on the lee side to steer. We are beating her," continued Waddie, when the Raven was a length ahead of her rival.

"But you will certainly drown us, Waddie!" cried Minnie, as the boat went down on the lee side to her washboard.

"If you will permit me to sit on the same side with you, Miss Wimpleton, I can relieve her a little," suggested Nick, as he rose from his place.

"Certainly, Mr. Van Wolter. Don't be so polite as to drown me."

Nick took a seat on the weather side, where he should have gone before. He again assured his fair companion that there was no danger, though he was really not so confident on this point as he pretended to be. He certainly was not afraid himself; on the contrary, he rather wished the boat would upset, and thus afford him the coveted opportunity to save Miss Wimpleton from the "watery grave." He could swim like a fish, and Waddie was so disabled that he could do no more than help himself. But the two boats dashed on, and the Raven did not go over. She soon ran away from the Belle, though it was done at the expense of a severe trial to Miss Minnie's nerves.

"Take in the jib, Nick," said Waddie. "The point is settled. The Raven is the fastest boat on the lake."

The willing assistant obeyed this order, and the boat went along a little steadier, much to the satisfaction of the young lady passenger.

"I hope you have not injured your coat, Mr. Van Wolter," said she, as he resumed his seat.

"Not at all, though it would be of no consequence if I had," replied Nick.

"I think it would. When a young gentleman has a really elegant appearance, it breaks my heart to see it disturbed."

"Your heart is very tender, Miss Wimpleton."

"Like all ladies' hearts."

Nick sighed.

Minnie laughed.

"What a beautiful breast-pin you wear, Mr. Van Wolter!"

"Do you like it?"

"I think it is lovely."

Nick put his hands up to take it out of the cravat, in order to make her a present of it; but he happened to remember, in season to save it, that it was the rose, and not the breast-pin, he was to give her, if she admired it. She did not allude to the flower, and all opportunities seemed to elude his grasp. It was provoking that the Raven would not upset, and afford him a chance to do a gallant deed. He thought Miss Minnie was in a very agreeable frame of mind. She spoke very kindly to him, and smiled with the utmost sweetness; for his vanity did not permit him to realize that she was making fun of him. If an opportunity could only be presented for him to do a big thing, — to tear her from the jaws of death, — all would be well with him, and, he was conceited enough to believe, with her also.

Waddie came about, and threw the boat up into the wind, to wait for the Belle. The Raven had fully justified her builder's promise, and the owner was satisfied. Tom Walton was nettled at his signal defeat. He could not quite understand it; so he did just what other smart boatmen do under similar circumstances — he declared that it was not the right breeze for the Belle. She was a heavy-weather boat, and he should like to catch the Raven out when it blew a fresh breeze. He would either beat her or drown her.

Waddie thought they had a pretty stiff breeze, but he would be happy to accommodate Tom on his own terms. The two boats sailed along together towards their destination. Waddie's shoulder troubled him, after the exercise he had taken, and he gave up the helm to Nick. The wind had gradually subsided until it was a dead calm off the South Shoe. The great black clouds had been travelling steadily towards the zenith, till the sun was obscured, and the aspect of the weather was decidedly threatening. Waddie looked at the rolling black clouds, and declared there was wind in them.

"What do you mean by that, Waddie?" asked Minnie, anxiously.

"We may have a squall," replied he, coolly.

"A squall!" exclaimed she, terrified by the word. "Do let us get ashore."

"A squall is nothing, if you only mind your eye," added the young boatman, lightly.

"But I am afraid of squalls," persisted Minnie. "Can't we go on shore?"

"Not very conveniently, as the shore is half a mile distant, and there is not a breath of wind. Don't be alarmed, Minnie. I have been out in twenty squalls, and really there is nothing to fear, if the boat is well handled."

"Look out for a squall!" shouted Tom Walton from the Belle, which had fallen astern as the breeze died out.

"Ay, ay!" replied Waddie. "I see it."

A squall! After all, there might be a chance for Nick to do a great deed in behalf of the fair passenger. It was evident enough that the Raven would go over with the slightest excuse for doing so. As Waddie said nothing about it, he did not deem it incumbent upon him to suggest the propriety of taking in sail. His mother told him to "make a chance." It was wicked to do so, and perhaps it was involuntarily that he put several half hitches in the mainsheet, as he made it fast to the cleat.

"If we can get a puff or two of wind, we can run up to the South Shoe, and anchor," said Waddie.

"It's coming!" shouted Tom Walton, whose quick eye had already discovered the approach of the squall.

"Yes, there it comes," added Waddie, quietly. "I'll take the helm, Nick; you may go forward and stand by the halyards."

"I will," replied Nick.

"Don't let go till I tell you," continued Waddie. "It may not come here, and a capful of wind will take us to the shore."

"Say when you are ready," added Nick, as he stationed himself on the half deck.

The tempest drove down the lake, piling up great billows before it, stirring up the sleet and spray in its path, till the shore was hid from the gaze of the voyagers.

"Look out for it!" roared Tom Walton, whose voice could scarcely be heard above the noise of the wind and waters.

He had lowered the mainsail of the Belle half way down, so that the light puffs which came before the squall drove her almost up to the spot where the Raven lay motionless on the still waters.

"Let go the halyards!" shouted Waddie, sharply. "Be lively about it! The squall is upon us!"

"Down with your mainsail!" cried Tom, as the blast swept down upon the Raven. "Let go your sheet!"

By this time the Belle's mainsail was down, with a couple of stops on to secure it to the boom. Waddie had already, with his single serviceable hand, sprung to the quarter to let go the sheet. The half hitches which Nick had put in the rope bothered him, and his fingers seemed to be all thumbs. The wind began to swell the sail, and increased the difficulty of the operation, while Nick seemed to be having no little trouble in detaching the halyards.

"Let go! Down with the mainsail!" cried Waddie, furiously.

"Ay, ay!" replied Nick, as he let go the halyards; but he was just half a second too late.

The squall struck the sail, and the Raven toppled over as easily as though she had been built for the express purpose of upsetting. In an instant Miss Minnie was floundering in the mad waves, and screaming for help. The glorious opportunity to do a noble deed, for which Nick had so devotedly hoped, had come. Waddie was thrown into the water, but he clung to the boom with his uninjured arm.

Unfortunately for Nick, his legs were tangled in the halyards of the sail. The Raven's ballast shifted, and she rolled over till she lay bottom upwards on the waves. Nick was drawn under water by the action of the boat; but he quickly freed his legs

from the rope, and coming up, clung to the hull till he could ascertain the position of Miss Minnie, who was still struggling in the waves some distance from the boat.

He was too late. The circumstances mocked him again. The squall was subsiding, and Tommy Toppleton, like a true knight, had leaped into the water the instant he saw Minnie's condition, and was swimming towards her. The glorious opportunity was lost.

CHAPTER V.

ROMANCE AND REALITY.

THE squall was very brief in its duration, lasting hardly a minute; but it was immediately followed by torrents of rain. Tommy Toppleton was a strong swimmer, and having but a short distance to make, he soon reached the spot where Minnie was vainly struggling. She was nearly exhausted by the violence of her useless efforts, when Tommy grasped her in his arms, and lifted her head above the water. Half a minute later, the Belle came to his assistance, and Tom Walton drew the sufferer into the boat.

Mr. Nicholas Van Wolter was disgusted, and highly indignant that Tommy Toppleton should venture to perform the noble part which he had assigned to himself. All his brilliant prospects were imperilled, for not only had Nick lost the prestige of saving the fair being himself, but another had won it. The admiration, gratitude, and love which the rescue was to secure for him, had been wrested from him by the venturesome Tommy. His Sunday clothes had been wet for nothing, and he was even willing to believe that he had come nearer being drowned himself than any other member of the party.

The gallant Tommy was hastily assisted into the Belle, and Tom Walton headed her towards the wreck of the Raven, where Waddie and Nick were relieved from their uncomfortable situation. Minnie was in the little cuddy forward, with Grace Toppleton, who had retired to its friendly shelter before the squall came on. Strange as it may seem, these young ladies were hardly acquainted with each other, for the relations between their respective families had prevented them from meeting, except by accident. Once, since Tommy and Waddie had buried the hatchet, their sisters had been together for a few moments, and for the first time in their lives had spoken to each other. But Grace was all kindness and attention, and did all that the circumstances would admit for the comfort of Minnie.

"How is Minnie?" demanded Waddie, anxiously, as soon as he was helped into the boat.

"She is doing very well, I think," replied Tommy. "She was not in the water more than a couple of minutes, and her clothing buoyed her up so that she did not go down at all."

"You are a noble fellow, Tommy. You saved her life, and I shall always be grateful to you," added Waddie, grasping the hand of the hero.

"There wasn't any need of jumping overboard — not a bit," interposed Tom Walton, with his good-natured grin.

"I don't know that there was any need of it, but it seemed to me just as though something ought to be done at once," replied Tommy. "Our sails were down, and I was afraid she would sink before we could get to her in the boat."

"You did just what you thought was right, Tommy," added Tom Walton. "You were just as noble as George Washington himself; but, if you had taken the other oar, and helped me work the boat, we could have reached Miss Wimpleton just as quick, if not a little quicker, than you could swim to her."

The skipper of the Belle was a very practical young man. Perhaps his education had been neglected, for he had never read a romance in his life, and was utterly unable to appreciate the sublime heights to which Nick soared.

"If there was no need of jumping overboard, I am sorry I did it," said Tommy, laughing. "I did not suppose you could move the boat without hoisting the mainsail, and my idea was, that the young lady would drown before the Belle could be started. But Miss Wimpleton is safe, and we need not trouble ourselves any more about the matter."

"You did first rate, Tommy," replied Tom Walton; "but I hate to see a fellow risk his life when there isn't any need of it. That's all I wanted to say."

"By the great horn spoon, Tommy, you did the biggest thing a fellow ever did," said Waddie, with great enthusiasm.

"That's so," added Tom Walton. "He risked his life. I think just as much of the act as any of you, I want you to understand; but there wasn't any need of it."

"I did what I thought was best," repeated Tommy. "We won't say anything more about it now. What shall we do?"

"We will run over to Grass Springs, and the girls can dry themselves at the hotel," suggested Waddie.

"Good! Run for Grass Springs, Tom," said Tommy Toppleton.

"All right," answered the skipper, as he hoisted his mainsail; and in a few moments the Belle was headed towards the place indicated.

The rain continued to pour down in torrents, and Tom Walton, who had not been overboard, was just as wet as those who had been. Grace, in the cabin, was the only dry one of the party. But the boys had been so often ducked that they did not heed it. Under the gentle ministrations of Grace, Minnie recovered from the terror of the accident, and regained her self-possession.

"Your brother is a noble fellow," said she. "I am sure I should have sunk in another instant, if he had not come to my assistance."

"I am very glad Tommy was able to help you," replied Grace.

"I want to see him, and thank him for what he did," added Minnie.

"I will call him."

Tommy came at the summons, dripping like an eel just from his native element.

"Miss Wimpleton wishes to see you," said Grace, as he crawled into the cabin.

"I do, Mr. Toppleton. I must thank you for saving my life. I shall remember you with gratitude as long as I live."

"O, not at all, Miss Wimpleton. I only did what I thought was right, and I hope you won't feel under any obligations to me," replied Tommy, lightly.

"But I do feel under very great obligations to you, for I value my life very highly. I should certainly have been drowned if you had not come when you did."

"Tom Walton says there was not the least need of my jumping overboard," laughed the hero of the hour.

"I don't care what Tom Walton says; I shall always feel that I owe my life to you."

"O, no! Not quite so bad as that. Tom would have saved you in half a minute more, if I hadn't."

"You need not try to disparage what you have done; and if Tom Walton or anybody else does so, I shall hate him as long as I live."

"Nick Van Wolter says he was just going to swim

to you when he saw me close beside you; so you could not have drowned."

"Well, I am so thankful I owe my life to you, instead of Nick!" exclaimed Minnie, with a candor which did not pause to consider the possible consequences of such an admission.

"I am very much obliged to you for your good opinion, Miss Wimpleton. I'm sure you don't inherit the family rancor."

"Indeed, I do not! I used to hate all the Toppletons; but Waddie says you are a splendid fellow, though he did not find it out 'till since he made up with you."

"I am very much obliged to him," answered Tommy. "I know I used to be a pretty hard boy; but I have been trying to do better, and I am sure your good opinion will be a great encouragement to me."

"I don't know that my good opinion will do you much good; but I shall always think of you as a noble fellow, who risked his own life to save mine."

"I can only try to merit your esteem and regard," replied Tommy, as he gazed with an unwonted interest at the fair face and graceful form of Minnie.

"I don't think I shall ever dare to get into a boat again," added she, with something like a shudder. "At least, I shall not unless I know you are near, Mr. Toppleton."

"I don't exactly understand how the Raven was upset. Waddie is one of the best skippers on the lake," replied Tommy.

"He has a lame arm, you know."

"That boat went over very easy."

"I certainly will never get into that boat again. Where are we going now?"

"Over to the hotel at Grass Springs. You can dry yourself there, and then we will have some dinner," answered Tommy, as he left the cabin.

"Your brother is a real nice young man," said Minnie, as the subject of her remark disappeared.

"I think so myself, though he was not always so. Now he is kind and obliging to me, and to all the family. He would do anything for us, and never speaks a rude word, or does an ugly thing."

"It's just so with Waddie. Isn't it strange what a change has come over both of them?"

"Very strange, indeed; but what a blessed change

it is! A year ago, Tommy would not even let me go in a boat with him, though I am very fond of sailing."

"It was just so with Waddie. Now he invites me very often, though he has had the Raven only a few days. I hope he will have a safer boat. Do you know how my brother happened to become such a good boy?" inquired Minnie, suddenly raising her head and gazing earnestly at her companion, as though a new idea had flashed upon her mind. "I'll tell you. It was Captain Wolf Penniman that did it. Pooh! you needn't blush, Miss Toppleton."

"I was not aware that I did blush," added Grace, with some confusion.

"They say he is very fond of you."

"He is a very good friend of mine."

"I knew it," said Minnie, archly. "What does your father say about it?"

"My father?"

"Yes."

"About what?"

"About Wolf, of course."

"He thinks very highly of him, and is grateful to him for his kindness to Tommy when he was sick."

"But what does he say about you and Wolf?"

"About Wolf and me! Why, nothing, of course," replied Grace, evidently astonished at the remark.

"How dull you are!" laughed Minnie. "Everybody says Wolf is in love with you, and that you are not indifferent towards him."

"Why, I never thought of any such thing!" exclaimed Grace. "We are very good friends — that's all."

"Well, I suppose that's enough."

"Wolf was always very kind and very polite to me, and I think he is a very good and a very smart young man. I never had any other thought in regard to him."

"How people do talk!"

"Why, I'm only sixteen years old!"

"Sweet sixteen!"

"I don't think boys and girls of our age ought to meddle with such matters."

"Don't you?"

"Indeed I don't!"

"Does Wolf think so?"

"I don't know; but I'm certain that he never spoke of such things to me."

"Perhaps he will one of these days, when the time comes."

It was plain that Minnie had devoted more attention to a certain class of subjects than Grace had; but then she was nearly a year older. It was a question with her whether Major Toppleton would permit the young steamboat captain to entangle the affections of his daughter; for he could hardly permit her to become the wife of a common mechanic's son, even though he was the commander of a lake steamer. But, however different the views of the two young ladies in regard to these trying subjects, they were rapidly becoming the most devoted friends.

When the Belle reached the shore at Grass Springs, Tommy had made up his mind that Minnie was one of the prettiest girls he had ever seen, and he wondered that he had not discovered the fact before, for he had occasionally met her since the healing of the rupture between himself and her brother. Tommy was not quite eighteen, but he was progressive in his ideas.

CHAPTER VI.

A DISCOMFITED ASPIRANT.

"WHAT next?" asked Waddie Wimpleton, when the Belle was made fast to the wharf at Grass Springs.

"I will get a carriage to convey the ladies to the hotel," proposed Tommy. "And, while they are drying their clothes, we will go back and pick up the Raven."

"That will do it," replied Waddie. "We can order dinner at the same time. The sun is coming out, and we shall all be dry enough by the time we return."

Tommy soon procured a covered vehicle, and handed Miss Minnie to a seat within it. He appeared to be much interested in the young lady, and Mr. Nicholas Van Wolter watched him with a keen eye. It was natural enough that he should be so, and equally natural that the young lady should smile sweetly upon him, as she certainly did. According to Nick's theory, the parties were already in love; and, in his own heart, he abused the stars that had deprived him of the glorious opportunity which he had supposed was within his grasp. He had "made the chance," in the language of his ambitious mother, but another had gathered the fruit. He was sorely disappointed and disheartened at his ill luck. He had beaten the bush, but Tommy Toppleton had caught the game.

Nothing could rob him of the satisfaction of remembering that Minnie had smiled upon him, had spoken kindly to him, and had hinted at her admiration of him. Something might yet occur to turn the current in his favor, and all he could do at present was to watch his chances. He wished Tommy Toppleton was somewhere else, for it vexed him; and, in the language of the literature he patronized, "wrung the cords of his soul" to see his rival handing the fair one into the carriage, and to see her, dripping like a mermaid from the depths of the sea, smiling so significantly upon him.

It was agreed that Tommy should go up to the hotel with the ladies, and make the necessary arrangements for their accommodation, and for dinner for the whole party. It gave Nick an additional pang to see the hero of the day seat himself opposite the moist divinity, where he could gaze unrestrained into her face; and still another to observe that Miss Wimpleton seemed to be pleased with his company. It was a plain case, and the houses of Wimpleton and Toppleton were in imminent danger of being united by a marriage at no very distant day.

"Do you want to sell that boat of yours, Waddie?" said Tom Walton, as the carriage drove off, and the rest of the party seated themselves in the sun, which was now shining brightly, to dry their wet garments.

"What will you give for her?" replied Waddie, jocosely.

"Fifty cents."

"Won't you say seventy-five?"

"No; I wouldn't give more than half a dollar."

"The Raven is the fastest boat on the lake, since she has beaten the Belle handsomely."

"She beats her tipping over," laughed Tom.

"That wasn't her fault," replied Waddie, seriously "The Belle would have gone over under the same circumstances."

5

"I don't know but she would with the mainsail up and the sheet fast," answered Tom. "I suppose your lame arm prevented you from letting go the sheet."

"I suppose it did; but I don't usually fasten a sheet as that one was," said Waddie, glancing at Nick.

"Wasn't it fastened right?" asked Nick, rather diffidently.

"It was fastened to hold, but not to let go," replied Waddie, more sharply than he was in the habit of speaking of late. "Boatmen don't often put three or four hitches in a sheet, especially when there is a squall coming up. Did you intend to have the Raven upset?"

"Intend it?" stammered Nick.

"Yes, I asked you if you intended to upset the boat?"

"What makes you think I intended to upset her?" whined the culprit.

"Because, if you did, you went to work just right, and accomplished your purpose."

"Come, come, that's rather rough on a fellow," interposed Tom Walton, with a deprecatory grin. "Of course no fellow would intend to upset a boat when there was a lady in it."

"Do you put three or four half hitches on the cleat when you make fast your main sheet, Tom?" demanded Waddie, who was justly indignant at the discovery he had made just as the Raven upset — so indignant that he could not trust himself to speak of the matter in the presence of the ladies.

"Of course not. I never fasten the sheet at all when the wind is heavy or flawy. I always pass it over the cleat, and hold the end in my hand," answered the skipper of the Belle.

"That's the right way; and I have told Nick more than once, when he has been sailing with me, never to fasten the sheet, not even in a dead calm. When I went to cast off the sheet, I found three hitches at least, and I don't know but four or five, hauled up so tight that I could not loose them."

"But you don't believe Nick intended to have the squall upset the boat when it came — do you?"

"Of course I don't believe it."

Nick breathed easier.

"Because he was in the boat himself. It stands to reason a fellow don't want to upset the boat in which he is himself a passenger," argued Tom.

"Well, I only said if he had intended to upset her, he could not have done anything different from what he did. I don't mean to accuse him of anything out of the way," explained Waddie.

"I always like to do a thing well, and I suppose I overdid it this time," muttered Nick.

"I don't think, if I had had two hands to work with, I could have cast off the sheet in season to save the boat," continued Waddie.

"I can't imagine what you were thinking about when you fastened that sheet, Nick."

"I really don't know, myself," pleaded the culprit.

"Neither can I understand why you didn't let go the halyards when I told you to do so."

"I couldn't unfasten them. The ropes were new, and full of kinks," replied he.

"You hoisted the sail and secured the halyards yourself."

"I know I did; I don't pretend to be much of a sailor."

"But you have been in a boat enough to know how to handle one; and a fellow ought to be able to untie his own knots," continued Waddie.

"Well, what's done can't be helped," said the good-natured Tom Walton. It's no use to cry for spilled milk."

"But it's better to understand the matter, so as not to spill any more."

Waddie had no idea that his assistant had intended to upset the boat, though he rubbed very closely in his remarks upon the subject. The conduct of Nick seemed to be either criminal or inexcusably stupid. The Raven was disparaged, and he defended her when he exposed the bungling work of his companion. Indeed, when any one is careless with a boat, he ought to be severely censured; and Waddie, without malice, and only with a reasonable indignation, felt it to be his duty to express himself very plainly. The return of Tommy from the hotel put an end to the discussion, and the party embarked in the Belle to recover the wreck of the Raven.

They found her near the South Shoe, towards which she had drifted till her masts struck the sands of the shoal water. She did not carry ballast enough to sink her when she filled, and her cuddy had been closed when the accident happened, so that a portion of air remained to assist in buoying her up. She had turned into a nearly inverted position; but when the mast struck the bottom of the lake, the boat had continued to drift, till she was thrown up nearly on her beam ends. With the aid of a boat-hook, a rope was passed under the topmast, and the end carried in the Belle to the other side of the hull, which lay parallel with the line of shore. The Belle was then anchored, and all hands heaved on the rope till the Raven was brought to an upright position.

Both boats were supplied with buckets and baling dippers, and, after an hour's hard work, she was relieved of the load of water she contained, sponged out, and the sun soon dried her seats, so that she was in as good order as when she left Centreport in the morning. As soon as the party went on board of her, Waddie called the attention of the others to the manner in which the sheet was secured. There were four half hitches on the cleat, and even Tom Walton was forced to admit that Nick was crazy, or had intended to upset the boat. It was charitable to believe that he had lost his wits.

"I should not care a straw about it if Minnie had

not been frightened out of a year's growth," said Waddie.

"It is lucky she is pretty tall now," added Tom.

"She will never dare to sail in this boat again."

"We will explain it to her," suggested Tom.

"And let her understand that it was all Nick's fault," continued Waddie, roguishly; for, without comprehending the magnitude of the aspiring young gentleman's intentions, he knew that he had manifested a strong admiration for his sister.

Poor Nick could not say a word. His precious scheme for winning the favor of Minnie had resulted in covering him with odium and disgrace in her eyes. The day seemed to be absolutely lost, though he was brave enough to hope that the future would redeem his chances. Tommy Toppleton had won the day without any hard thought, without any difficult scheming. He was the glorious hero in Miss Wimpleton's estimation. She had bestowed sweet smiles on the fortunate fellow. Now, Waddie was going over to tell her that the unhappy Mr. Van Wolter had been the sole cause of all the mischief. The owner of the Raven would win back her reputation as a safe boat at his expense. He could not afford to quarrel with the little magnate; so he was obliged to be meek and submissive; but he did not wish to appear again that day in the presence of the injured divinity.

"I suppose I shall not be wanted any more to-day," said he, humbly.

"I think not; but you shall dine with us at the hotel," replied Waddie.

"I thank you; I don't want any dinner. I think I have taken cold. I don't feel very well. My digestion is out of order," stammered Nick. "If it is all the same to you, I would rather go home. I will take the next train at the Springs for Middleport."

"I don't want you to go back without your dinner, Nick," added Waddie, more gently; and his assistant was so humble that he began to think he had been too severe.

"I really don't want any dinner. I hope you will excuse me. I made a very bad blunder in the boat, and I know you all despise me, and that the ladies will despise me too," pleaded Nick.

"I won't say anything about the boat to them," added Waddie. "I was only joking when I spoke of telling Minnie it was your fault. I will forgive you if you will promise never to put even a single hitch in a sheet again."

"I never will. On my honor, I never will. It was a bad mistake; but it shall never be repeated. Really I would rather go home."

"Why don't you let him take your boat up, and you return with us?" suggested Tommy.

"Can you take the Raven up to Centreport without upsetting her, Nick?" asked Waddie.

"Certainly I can."

"Then you may take her."

"Thank you," replied Nick, as he hastened to set the mainsail.

Pushing off from the Belle, the discomfited Nick headed his craft up the lake.

"I'll bet there will be music in Grass Springs this afternoon," muttered he, shaking his head, as he saw the other boat fill away on her course.

CHAPTER VII.

COLONEL WIMPLETON DROPS THE REINS.

THE breeze was light after the shower, and the Raven did not give Nick Van Wolter much trouble to manage her. He was able, therefore, to devote his undivided thought to the disappointment he had experienced, and the odium he had incurred. Tommy Toppleton had stepped between him and the richest prize that ever lured a mortal young man; and Nick seemed to have no doubt that the treasure would have been easily won if his brilliant scheme had not miscarried. He did not thank Tommy for what he had done, and he envied him in the enjoyment of Miss Minnie's smile.

But one was a Toppleton and the other was a Wimpleton. The two houses had been at war for many years, and the two heads of the families were still as implacable and bitter as ever towards each other.

Major Toppleton would not permit his daughter to become a Wimpleton; and Colonel Wimpleton would not permit his daughter to share the lot of a Toppleton. Nick found consolation in this reflection. Yet it was a fact that Tommy and Minnie would dine and spend the day together. With the perversity of young men and young women under such circumstances, they would meet again without the knowledge of their fathers, and in a short time the matter would have gone so far that it could not be checked.

What would Colonel Wimpleton say if he knew that his daughter was filled with admiration and gratitude towards the son of his great enemy? Would he allow them to spend a whole day together? Certainly not. But he, the disinterested Mr. Nick Van Wolter, knew all about it. He was well aware that Tommy and Minnie were cementing an attachment which fathers could not break off. As a friend of the family, as a sincere well-wisher of Miss Wimpleton, was it not his duty to interfere, and inform the colonel of the nature of the proceedings at Grass Springs? He had no difficulty in convincing himself that such a course was the highest duty of the hour, and that it would be inexcusable in him to neglect to perform it,

Yet it was a disagreeable duty. Any interference on his part might cost him the valuable friendship of Waddie, though it might secure to him the more valuable influence of the colonel himself. As he considered the subject in all its bearings, he found himself very unwilling to incur the displeasure of Waddie, and, at the same time, of Minnie herself. It would ruin all his possible chances in the future. He had fully intended from the first that there should be "music" at Grass Springs that afternoon, and that Colonel Wimpleton should make it; but when he looked the matter fair in the face, he was not disposed to become the informer in person.

The colonel must know what was going on at the Springs. It was not prudent for Nick to tell him, and he thought of various expedients to accomplish the purpose. He could invent nothing that was quite satisfactory, though he had been nearly two hours in the boat considering this subject alone. He finally concluded to consult his mother, who was a veritable female Talleyrand in the art of diplomacy. This disposition of the matter did not suit him much better, inasmuch as he could not see how she was to manage the matter without implicating him.

While he was still arguing the case with himself, adopting and then rejecting various methods, the Raven's keel ground roughly on the sands at the bottom, and then came to a sudden stop. As the wind was not exactly fair to go up the lake, he had been obliged to beat, making a long and a short tack. The Raven had passed clear of a headland, about half way between Ruoara and Centreport, and was standing into a little bay above the point. Nick had been so absorbed in his reflections, that he did not notice the rapid shoaling of the water as he neared the shore. He immediately let go the sheet, in which he had put no half hitches this time; and seizing an oar, he attempted to push the boat off the shallow beach. But she had taken the ground while under full headway, and all his strength was not sufficient to move her.

In vain he pushed and swayed the boat; her keel was buried in the sand, and it was impossible for him to move her a single inch. He labored, sweat, and swore till he was heartily discouraged. The water was not knee deep over the bow, and rolling up the legs of his pants, he stood upon the bottom, and tried to pry her off with the oar; but in this task he was also unsuccessful. He was still three miles from home, and he did not like to walk this distance, on the one hand, or to endure the censure and criticism of Waddie, on the other, if he exposed his mismanagement to him. The road from Centreport to Ruoara lay close to the shore, and there was a house within a quarter of a mile of the spot. He finally concluded to go in search of assistance, for with the help of one or two others he could push the Raven off into deep water.

Taking his shoes and stockings in his hand, he waded ashore, and, having put them on, he started for the nearest house, in the direction of Ruoara. He had gone but a few steps before he was startled by the appearance of a buggy coming towards him, the horse attached to which was running at the top of his speed. His first impulse was to get out of the road, and let the frightened animal go on his way to destruction, with the helpless gentleman who occupied the seat of the vehicle. But a second glance assured him that the individual in the buggy was Colonel Wimpleton. Possessed of the current information in regard to the personal habits of the magnate of Centreport, Nick had no difficulty in satisfying himself that the great

man was intoxicated, and had lost the control of the spirited animal he drove. Perhaps this was the chance which had long been in store for the ambitious young man.

Perhaps it would serve his turn as well to save the father as the daughter. But it was no easy matter to stop a terrified horse, though, if the stars were favorable, he might succeed in doing it. Nick had only one instant for reflection; if he had had two, very likely he would have declined to attempt the perilous feat. Impelled only by the desire to do a big thing in the service of the powerful and influential man of Centreport, he pulled off his coat and commenced flourishing it furiously in the middle of the road. The horse saw this obstacle in his path, and evidently did not like the looks of it. He snorted wildly, and exhibited an evident intention to dodge it. Sheering towards the lake, he attempted to pass the obstruction; but Nick changed his position, and the animal abated his headlong speed.

"Stop him! Stop him!" cried the colonel, who was plainly terrified by the situation, for the reins were dragging on the ground.

The horse, intimidated by this movement on the part of Nick, threw himself back upon the breeching with such force as to pitch the colonel forward upon the dasher of the buggy. The mad animal snorted furiously in his terror, and then seemed disposed to wheel and run in the opposite direction; but the instant his speed was checked, Nick dropped his coat and sprang to the bridle of the horse. It was the coat, and not the young man, which had frightened the animal; and when this was no longer before him, he attempted to renew his flight towards home, and dragged poor Nick for twenty rods before he could produce any effect by his bold action.

Having once grasped the bridle rein, Nick was obliged to hold on for his own safety; for if he let go, he was sure to be thrown down and mangled under the wheels. The horse had not yet broken into a run after his flight was checked, and, dragging Nick by his bit, he was not likely to do so till he had shaken off this burden. By the dint of tugging and jerking, the young man had drawn the horse's head round to one side, which impeded his efforts to go forward. The animal was not ugly, but frightened, and his struggles were only honest efforts to escape.

"Whoa, Major; whoa!" said Nick, in soothing tones, for he had had some experience with horses.

By these gentle means he succeeded in quieting the animal, and finally in stopping him, though he was still quivering with terror, and very impatient of restraint.

"Whoa, Major; whoa!" continued Nick, panting from the violence of his own efforts.

He had learned the horse's name at the owner's stable; and patting him on the neck, he soon reduced him to a state of tolerable calmness. Colonel Wimpleton improved the earliest opportunity to get out of the buggy. It was plain enough that he had been drinking a great deal; but the perils through which he had passed had done something to modify the influence of his drams.

"You have done me a good turn, young man," said the magnate, when he was safe on the solid ground.

"Whoa, Major; whoa!" added Nick, as the horse began to be impatient again.

"O, it's Nick Van Wolter!" exclaimed the colonel, as he recognized the person to whom he was indebted for this signal service.

"Yes, sir; that is my name," replied Nick. "The Major is wide awake to-day."

"I never knew him to attempt to run away before. I don't know exactly how it was; but in brushing a fly from his flank, I dropped the reins. While I was trying to get them again, he got frightened, and broke into a run," added the colonel.

Nick was not so impolitic and impolite as to hint at the true explanation; but probably the great man, overcome by his frequent cups, had dropped asleep, and lost the reins from his grasp; and doubtless they had dangled against the horse's heels, and terrified him. This was the most probable solution of the problem.

"Yes, sir; I did that same thing once myself, when I was driving the mail wagon; but my horse was not smart enough to run away," replied Nick, wishing to do all he could to soften the mortification of the great man. "Whoa, Major; whoa. Stand still; that's a good fellow!"

"You have done me a good turn, young man," added the colonel, who felt compelled to express his obligations.

"I'm glad to serve you, sir," answered Nick, struggling to be modest.

"Come to my house, when you get back to town, and I will make it all right with you."

"O, it's all right now, sir."

"Not quite," said the colonel. "You have done well; but this will be a good day's work for you. You shall be well paid for what you have done."

"I don't want any pay, sir, for doing a thing like this," replied Nick, in the words of the romances he had read.

"Come and see me, at any rate."

"I will, sir, if you desire; but I don't wish to be paid for a slight service like this."

"Won't you ride home with me?" added the colonel, as he stepped into the buggy, the horse being by this time apparently quite reconciled.

"Thank you, sir; I have a boat here."

"Very well; but come and see me as soon as you return;" and the magnate started his horse.

CHAPTER VIII.

SECRETS FOR TWO.

"I HAVE done a big thing now, anyhow!" exclaimed Nick to himself, as the great man of Centreport drove off.

But the buggy had proceeded but a short distance before it stopped. Colonel Wimpleton had forgotten something which he wished to say or do, and Nick hastened back to ascertain what more he could do for him.

"Is anything the matter, sir?" asked Nick, as he rushed up to the vehicle.

"No; nothing. I want to say a word to you, young man, before I go," said the colonel, whose expression was sheepish and embarrassed.

"Yes, sir," answered Nick, as the speaker paused.

"You are, no doubt, a very discreet young man," continued the colonel.

"I try to be so, sir."

"I don't like to be talked about."

"No one does, sir."

"By the merest accident in the world I dropped my reins, and my horse ran away with me."

"It was only what might happen to any one, sir."

"Very true."

"Even to the minister, if he drove a smart horse," suggested Nick, who exactly comprehended the meaning of the great man.

"Certainly; but people talk more about what I do and say than they do about other folks."

"Your high position and vast influence make you very prominent in the community, sir. It is not strange they should talk about you."

"Perhaps not; but I don't like to be misapprehended."

In other words, Colonel Wimpleton feared if people knew his horse ran away with him, that they would think he had been drinking too much. He was morbidly sensitive in regard to his besetting vice; and though there was hardly a man, woman, or child within ten miles of Centreport who had not heard that he drank too much, he supposed only a few intimate friends suspected his infirmity. Like all tipplers of his description, he did not believe that he was ever actually intoxicated.

"I understand you precisely, sir," added Nick. "Nothing happens to any one around here but somebody says he was drunk."

Colonel Wimpleton frowned.

"Of course, no one can suspect you of. anything of that sort, unless he belongs on the other side of the lake," continued Nick, taking due notice of the frown.

"In a word, young man, you need not mention that my horse ran away to-day," said the colonel.

"Certainly not, sir; I did not intend to mention it, unless you did so first yourself. I hope I understand my position better than to do such a thing."

"Keep your tongue still, and you shall not lose anything by it."

"I understand you, sir; and no one shall ever be the wiser for anything I say."

"That's right; come and see me as soon you return. What are you doing up here?"

"I have been down to Grass Springs with Waddie and Miss Minnie," answered Nick, who thought if he kept the colonel's secret, the colonel ought to keep his secret.

"Were they out in the boat?"

"Yes, sir; and Tommy Toppleton and Miss Grace were with them."

"Humph!" sneered the magnate, with a savage frown. "What are they doing there?"

"They are going to have a dinner at the hotel, and a good time generally, I suppose. We met with an accident going down, sir."

"What was that?"

"Waddie's boat capsized in the squall, and we were all pitched into the lake."

"What!" exclaimed the colonel, startled at the intelligence.

"But they are all safe, sir," added Nick, promptly. "Tommy Toppleton swam out and rescued Miss Minnie."

"She is safe, then," said the father, with a sigh of relief.

"O, yes! She is all right now. I didn't mean to

say anything to you about it, sir," continued Nick, fixing his eyes on the ground, as though he was mortified at the mistake he had made.

"Why didn't you mean to say anything to me about it?" demanded the colonel.

"Well, sir, only because I make it a point to mind my own business. If you will excuse me, I won't say any more. I did not intend to mention the subject."

"What do you mean? What is going on over there?"

"O, nothing, sir," replied Nick, in just that style of expression which assures the hearer there is a secret to be concealed. "I hope you will not mention the fact that I spoke of the affair, for I had no right to meddle with it."

"What affair? What are you talking about?" said the magnate, sharply.

"I ought not to have said that the boat was upset."

"Why not?"

"Because Tommy Toppleton saved Minnie. But I hope you won't ask me to say anything more about it," pleaded Nick.

"What more is there to be said?"

"Nothing, sir."

"Yes, there is!" protested the colonel, his curiosity excited to the highest pitch.

"You and Major Toppleton don't agree very well together, sir; and, so far as you are concerned, I don't wonder at it. Of course Miss Minnie is very grateful to Tommy; but, really, I must not say anything more. I shall ruin myself with Waddie and Miss Minnie, if they find that I have spoken to you about a matter which does not concern me."

"Don't you be alarmed, young man; I will not mention to any one that I have even seen you," replied the colonel, more gently. "If you have anything to say, speak out."

"I don't like to say anything; but I couldn't help thinking all the morning that you would be very angry if you knew what was going on."

"What is going on?" demanded the great man, his patience exhausted by the apologies and explanations of Nick.

"Well, sir, one of these days, your daughter, Miss Minnie, will be the wife of Tommy Toppleton," replied Mr. Van Wolter, desperately. "Of course I give it only as my opinion, and you can take it for what it is worth."

"The wife of Tommy Toppleton! Why, they are only children!" exclaimed the colonel.

"Tommy is a child of eighteen, and Miss Minnie is a child of sixteen," added Nick, shrugging his shoulders.

The magnate knit his brow. Fathers are the last to ascertain that their sons and daughters are men and women. He knew that Waddie and Tommy had been quite intimate for several months, and it was possible that the daughter might share these friendly relations. In his estimation, a matrimonial alliance between the two families would be a terrible thing.

"So Tommy saved Minnie's life," said the colonel, musing on the probabilities of the case.

"Not quite so bad as that. The Belle would have picked her up in a moment, if he had not gone to her assistance. I was on the point of swimming to her myself; but I got tangled up in the halyards, and was dragged under the boat when she upset.

Tom Walton said there was no need of Tommy's jumping overboard."

"But he did swim to her?"

"Yes; and Miss Minnie says he is a noble and generous fellow, and all that sort of thing. I saw how the matter was going, and I'll bet my life it will end in a ring."

"It shall not! I'll send Minnie to the other end of the world before any such thing shall happen," protested the colonel, wrathfully.

"Well, sir, I don't want to meddle with matters that do not concern me, but I thought you ought to know it," continued Nick. "I'm not quite sure that Waddie and Miss Grace are not a little sweet with each other, but I don't like to say anything."

"I am very glad you have spoken to me about this matter, Nick," said Colonel Wimpleton. "I think I have been a little blind. Waddie and Tom Toppleton have been together a great deal lately; and now, if the girls are going with them, there certainly will be mischief. I won't have it!"

"I knew you wouldn't, sir, if you only knew it; but I'm afraid I've made a great mistake in meddling with a matter which does not concern me. Waddie and Miss Minnie would hate me if they knew I had said anything to you."

"They shall not know it. No one shall know that you have even seen me to-day."

"They shall not know it from me," replied Nick, significantly.

"I won't have it!" repeated the colonel, musing upon the suspected relations between Tommy and his daughter, as he picked up the reins and started his horse.

"There'll be music over there this afternoon," muttered Nick, as he walked towards the house where he expected to obtain help in getting the Raven afloat.

Colonel Wimpleton drove a short distance, and then stopped. Drawing a flask from his breast pocket, he drank another dram. He had been to Ruoara to call upon a friend, with whom he had drank several times, and who had presented him this flask of brandy, because the colonel had praised it as a very superior article. His runaway horse had neutralized the effects of what he had taken in Ruoara; but the news given him by Nick had excited him, and under any excitement he drank more freely than usual. Before he reached home he had repeated the draught two or three times. His mind dwelt heavily upon the perils which threatened his family. Nick seemed so unwilling to say anything, that he concluded the case was much worse than he had described it. He was willing to believe that Waddie and Grace, Tommy and Minnie, had met before, and that a double union between the embittered houses was impending. He must put a stop to it without an hour's delay. Wolf Penniman was the intimate friend of both Waddie and Tommy; and the colonel had no difficulty in believing that he was their confidant and helpmate. In his tipsy condition he hastened on board of the Ucayga, which had just arrived from the foot of the lake. Wolf would know where the culprits were, and should go with him to the place.

Nick reached the house, towards which he had directed his steps, just after twelve o'clock. The "men folks" had come home to dinner, and the farmer's boys were willing to help him.

"Did you see anything of a runaway horse down the road, about an hour ago?" asked the farmer.

"Yes; I saw a horse hitched to a buggy going it at a pretty lively gait towards Centreport," replied Nick.

"Do you know what became of it?"

"The horse stopped on the hill below here. I suppose he got tired of running," answered Nick, cautiously.

"Do you know who it was?"

"No; he was a stranger to me."

"I was so far off I couldn't see very well; but it looked a little like Colonel Wimpleton's team."

"It wasn't the colonel's horse. He passed within a short distance of me. I know the colonel and his team very well. It wasn't he, I'm very sure," protested Nick, who could lie a little more easily than he could speak the truth.

"I didn't know but it might be Colonel Wimpleton. They say he steams it pretty hard now."

"It wasn't the colonel, I know; for I saw the man's face very distinctly. He was a younger man than the colonel."

The farmer was apparently satisfied, and the two young men accompanied Nick to the place where the Raven was aground. With their friendly aid she was soon floated in deep water, and headed towards Centreport, where she arrived just as the Ucayga was leaving the wharf on her down trip.

[We are ready to let Wolf continue his narrative, from the point where we left him, with Colonel Wimpleton lying on the track, between the rails. The choice brandy presented to him by his friend in Ruoara had been an evil spirit to him, not only inflaming his wrath against his son and daughter, but depriving him of the power to take care of himself. When the train stopped he had got out to ascertain the cause of the delay. The cars started, but he was too tipsy to reach the steps in season to get on board, and was left behind. He shouted, but no one heard him. He was vexed, and believing that brandy was the best medicine for vexation, he took a liberal dose of it from the flask. His repeated libations had impaired his locomotive powers to such an extent that he could hardly walk, and just as the train had backed down to him, his legs gave way, and he fell between the rails. But let Wolf proceed.]

CHAPTER IX.

THE TIPSY MAGNATE.

I WAS shocked and mortified to see my employer in such a terrible state of intoxication. He had been growing worse and worse from the moment he came into the state-room, on board of the Ucayga. He had narrowly escaped being crushed beneath the train, and my heart beat wildly as I realized the peril of his situation.

"What zye about, Wolfz?" said he, as I hastened to the assistance of the inebriate. "What'd zye go off and leave me here for — dzeh?"

"Why did you get out of the cars, sir?"

"To dzee what's the matter."

"Let me help you, sir."

"I don't zwant any help."

"Hurry up," said the conductor, from the platform of the rear car. The colonel tried to get up alone, but he could not. The brakeman and myself each took an arm, and lifted him up. With considerable difficulty, we got him into the car, for he seemed to have sense enough left to know that he was intoxicated, and was not willing to be assisted, lest it should be regarded as an acknowledgment of the fact. He apparently wished to conceal his condition, obvious as it was. We put him in his seat, and he tried to stiffen up his relaxed muscles, and appear like a sober man. If he had not been a pitiable spectacle, he would have been a ludicrous one; though many in the car, who had no special interest in his fate, laughed at his silly and stupid struggles to conceal his condition.

As talking was rather a difficult achievement for him, he kept still till the train arrived at Grass Springs. I told him we had reached our destination, and he rose unsteadily to his feet. He insisted upon walking alone, and repulsed all my efforts to assist him. By holding on to the chains and the railings on the platform, he succeeded in getting out of the car; but it was simply impossible for him to walk, and he would have fallen if I had not taken his arm. I called a carriage, and assisted him to a seat in it. People stared, smiled, and jeered at the magnate of Centreport in this unhappy condition, and I was glad enough to get him out of sight. I told the driver to convey us to the hotel, where I intended to take a private room for him, and let him sleep off the effects of his debauch, or, at least, keep out of sight until he was in condition to be seen.

Of the circumstances which had excited the indignation of Colonel Wimpleton I knew but little. He had somehow discovered that Waddie and Grace were together. I had ascertained that Tommy Toppleton had come down with Grace to meet Waddie on the Horse Shoe. They had started after the steamer left for Ucayga, and I had not seen their departure. I was to procure a boat, as I understood the plan, and convey the colonel to the island, where he could interfere with the "courting" which was alleged to be in progress; but in his present condition I had no idea of doing anything of the kind. I seated myself in the carriage with him.

"Now, where's — where's — yes — where's Waddie?" said he, with much difficulty; for he was so tipsy that his tongue almost refused to perform its office.

"I don't know where he is. We will go up to the hotel and inquire," I replied.

"That's zright — the hotel."

The driver, as I had directed him, stopped at the side door of the house, on his arrival. The landlord opened it, and I whispered to him that I wanted a private apartment for the colonel. With his assistance I conducted the drunken magnate to the room, and seated him on a sofa.

"Hadn't you better lie down, sir?" I asked, when the landlord had left me alone with him.

"Lie dzown!" exclaimed he, with a convulsive jerk of the head; "what for?"

"You don't seem to be very well to-day," I suggested.

"No; not — not very well. I've been dzick — dzick all day to-day. I took a little brandy for my — brandy for my stomach's sake," stammered he.

"Perhaps if you lie down you will feel better."

"I dzon't know — but you are right, Wolfz. I'm dzick. Did you dzell the folks — the folks on the dzrain that — I was — that I was — I was dzick?"

"No, sir; I did not tell them so; but they could

not help seeing that something was the matter with you."

"I dz'pose they did. I'll lie down, Wolfz."

He sprang to his feet, and, with a desperate effort, attempted to throw off his coat. He did not succeed, but pitched over upon his face on the bed. I pulled his coat off, while he lay in this position, and, rolling him over, placed him in as comfortable a posture as I could. After covering him with a blanket, I seated myself on the sofa, to consider the situation. I was unwilling to believe that the great man had ever been in such a deplorable condition before. His coat lay on the chair where I had thrown it. I could see the neck of the flask protruding from the pocket. I think I inherited from my mother a spite against bottles used to contain liquor. By this time the colonel was asleep, and I took the flask from the coat. It was about one third filled, and I had no doubt the inebriate had consumed the other two thirds. I went to the window, and poured it out upon the ground. I had once performed a similar service for my father, and I had no scruples in doing it for the magnate of Centreport, as he was, just then, by the force of circumstances, in my care. Screwing on the stopple of the flask, I restored it to the pocket where I had found it. My patient could now drink no more till he left the room.

He slept very soundly, snoring heavily in his drunken stupor. Slumber was the best thing in the world for him, and I left him "to fight it out on this line." I decided to take a boat and go over to the Horse Shoe, to ascertain for my own sake, rather than the colonel's, the nature of the relations which had so violently disturbed my employer. I had a pair of eyes, and I flattered myself I could tell, by his actions, whether Waddie had become suddenly interested in Grace. I knew that he had seldom seen her, and had hardly spoken to her since the reconciliation with her brother. But in such matters those who are most deeply concerned are often the blindest, and it was possible that my friend, and in some sense my *protégé*, had unwittingly stepped between me and my hopes.

Colonel Wimpleton would probably sleep soundly for a couple of hours, at least, and I went to the office to request the landlord to look out for him during my absence, and especially not to furnish him with any more liquor, if he could possibly avoid it.

"I'm going over to the Horse Shoe," I began.

"Didn't you come down to join the party here?" he asked, interrupting me.

"What party?"

"Why, the young gentlemen and young ladies."

"Whom do you mean?"

"Mr. Toppleton and Mr. Wimpleton."

"Are they here?" I replied.

"They have been here these two hours; the ladies longer than that."

"Who are the ladies?"

"Miss Wimpleton and Miss Toppleton."

"Is Miss Wimpleton here?" I inquired, gaining a crumb of comfort from the suggestion, for it might be Tommy and Minnie whose progressive tendencies had excited the alarm of the colonel.

"Yes, they are both here. They ordered dinner for six, but Tom Walton seems to be the only other person present."

"Don't tell them I am here, if you please," I added. "I wouldn't have Waddie and his sister see their father in his present condition for anything in the world."

"I never saw the colonel so bad before," said the landlord, shaking his head.

"He will sleep it off, after a while, I hope," I replied. "Then Waddie and Tommy are not on the Horse Shoe?"

"No; they were going there, and met with an accident."

"What was that?" I asked, with no little anxiety; for I could not forget that Grace was one of the party.

"The Raven upset in the squall this forenoon, and Miss Wimpleton came pretty near getting drowned."

"Indeed! Was Miss Toppleton with her?"

"No; she was in the Belle, with her brother. Tommy Toppleton jumped overboard, and swam to Miss Wimpleton's assistance, or it would have been all over with her. Tom Walton picked them up. The ladies came right over here, and my wife and daughters gave them some clothes, while they dried and ironed their own."

"I am glad they got out of the scrape so well."

"They were lucky."

"I didn't like the looks of that Raven, when she

came down from Hitaca," I added. "She didn't look as though she knew how to stay right side up."

"Tom Walton says the boat is crank, but it was not her fault. The other fellow with Waddie —"

"Who was that? — Nick Van Wolter?"

"Yes, that's the one. He put three or four half hitches in the main sheet, so that Waddie could not cast it off when the squall came up. They sent him back with the Raven; and I reckon they wanted to get rid of him," said the landlord, with a sly twinkle in his eye.

"Why so?"

"I suppose they did not like the looks of him, after he had caused the boat to be capsized," laughed mine host. "But I reckon that Tommy Toppleton is a little sweet with the Wimpleton girl, since he helped her out of the water."

I did not care to encourage the landlord in speaking on this delicate topic. I confess I was pleased to learn that there was nothing as yet to implicate Waddie in the "courting." I could not understand how Colonel Wimpleton had obtained his hint of these proceedings. Possibly he had no suggestion of them, except the fact that the party were at the Springs. Waddie had sent Nick Van Wolter home with the Raven, but I was confident she had not arrived when I left Centreport. I concluded that the colonel's suspicions simply grew out of his knowledge that his son and daughter were with the son and daughter of his great enemy.

I learned from the landlord that the party were then at dinner. I was anxious to know more of the relations of the suspected lovers; but I was fully determined to conceal from Waddie and his sister the fact that their father was in the house. The Belle was my boat, and Tom Walton had been running her on shares for me, intending to purchase her as soon as he was able to do so. He regarded himself as under great obligations to me, not only for the use of the boat, but because I had given him employment during the winter on board of the steamer. I could confide in him, and I asked the landlord to inform him privately that I was in the house, and wished to see him as soon as he had finished his dinner.

CHAPTER X.

TOM WALTON EXPRESSES HIS OPINION.

I KNEW that the mention of my name would bring Tom Walton to me, for he was one of the most devoted fellows in the world. He had a habit of remembering what a friend had done for him, and the manifestation of his gratitude was so profuse as to be rather embarrassing to me, for I did not like to see any one so weighed down by the burden of obligation as he appeared to be. I was in the room adjoining that in which I had put the colonel to bed; for I dared not expose myself where it was possible for Waddie, or any other member of the party except Tom, to see me, when he came to me.

"I didn't expect to see you here, Wolf," said he, his face lighted up with the broad grin which usually expressed his satisfaction at passing events. "Why don't you come in and take some dinner with Waddie and Tommy? I know they will be glad to see you."

"I should be very sorry to have them see me just now," I replied.

"Why, what's the matter? What's the row? Has anything broke?" he asked, a shade of anxiety overspreading his face.

"In a word, Tom, Colonel Wimpleton is as drunk as a beast, in the next room."

"Whew!" said, or rather whistled, Tom, his eyes opening till they looked like a couple of saucers.

"Yes; and he came within about a quarter of an inch of being run over and smashed by the train that brought us down."

"You don't say so!" exclaimed Tom, with genuine feeling.

"That's so. I wouldn't have Waddie or Miss Minnie see him now for all the money that he is worth."

"But I didn't know the colonel got so bad. I have heard people say he drank till he was about how-came-you-so: I never knew he got right down boozy."

"I never saw him so bad before," I replied; "and I hope I never shall again. It's really horrible."

"What are you doing down here with him, if he is so much over the bay?"

"He was not so bad when we started. He has been nursing on brandy ever since we left Centreport, and now he don't know himself from a bar of yellow soap. He is asleep, and I hope he will come out of it all right. I have emptied the contents of his bottle out the window."

"Good for you, Wolf!" said Tom, with an expressive grin.

I then told him all that had passed between the colonel and myself since he came into my state-room, on board of the steamer, dwelling particularly on the suspicions which had induced the magnate to visit Grass Springs. Tom smiled significantly as I proceeded, and I judged from his expression that he understood the case perfectly.

"Now, Tom, what does all this mean?" I asked, when I had finished the narrative.

"Well, I reckon the colonel is considerable more than half right," replied the skipper of the Belle, candidly.

"You really think that Waddie and Miss Grace are

interested in each other," I added, squarely, determined to know the worst, so far as I was personally concerned, at once.

"O, no! no! no!" protested Tom, vehemently, as his chin dropped down; "I don't mean anything of that sort."

He was much disturbed to think he had conveyed to me a wrong impression on a subject that so deeply affected me.

"What is it, then?"

"It's Tommy Toppleton and Miss Minnie;" and he proceeded to relate to me the particulars of the upsetting of the Raven, and of the gallant deed of Tommy.

"There wasn't the least need of jumping overboard; but Miss Minnie thinks her life was saved by it, and she is as grateful as though she had been pulled out of a burning fiery furnace. It's none of my business; so I don't say anything to her about it. I think she likes him, and he likes her. Between you and me, Wolf, she isn't a bad looking girl, and I don't blame Tommy."

"But he has hardly ever met her before to-day," I suggested.

"I don't care anything about that. Of course, they don't say anything, but I can tell by their looks which way the wind blows. I'll bet the biggest fish in the deepest water off Priam that something will come of it."

"I don't exactly understand how I took the idea from the colonel that it was Grace and Waddie who were getting things mixed," I added, laughing, to assure Tom that I had no feeling about the matter.

"O, no! Not a bit of it," protested the skipper, earnestly, shaking his head to emphasize his words. "Waddie behaves like a gentleman, of course; but, between us, he knows better than to look sidewise at Miss Grace."

"Why shouldn't he, if he is disposed to do so?"

"I reckon he knows a mill-stone from a hogshead of molasses," replied Tom, with his usual significant grin. "In the first place, he thinks too much of you to try to go to sea in your boat."

"My boat?"

"O, come, Wolf! What's the use of beating to windward when you have a fair breeze? You believe in Miss Grace, and she thinks a heap of you."

"We are very good friends; but she is the daughter of a wealthy man, while I am the son of a mechanic," I replied, rather gloomily.

"I don't care for that," said Tom, with a show of indignation at the vain distinctions of this world. "It will come out all right."

"I don't know," I answered, not caring to discuss the subject at any greater length; "Colonel Wimpleton is very much disturbed about the courting, as he calls it."

"How should he know anything about it?" demanded Tom, suddenly, as he recalled the circumstances of the day.

"I don't know."

"Did that Nick Van Wolter tell him?"

"No; he had not returned with the Raven when we left Centreport."

"If he did, I should be willing to break his head on my own account."

"I think the colonel ascertained that the girls had come down with the boys, and imagined all the rest," I suggested, giving the explanation which I had myself adopted.

"Well, he imagined it about right, then," said Tom.

"I am not sorry it is as you say; but I am afraid the affair will make a good deal of trouble. When are you going back?"

"Whenever my party says the word."

"Can't you hurry them up?" I inquired, anxiously; for I did not like to have Waddie and his sister in the house with their father, under the present circumstances.

"I don't know but I can. They were going to the Horse Shoe this afternoon," answered Tom. "I have been looking for another shower to-day, for 'thunder in the morning bids the sailor take warning.'"

There were as yet no signs of another shower, and the skipper left me to ascertain whether his party intended to visit the Horse Shoe or not. I carefully opened the door, and entered the colonel's room. He was still sleeping in the stupor of intoxication, and I left him. I wished to be at Centreport in season to take the steamer at half past five, but I was afraid my patient would not be in a condition to go home by the last train. Tom soon returned to me with the intelligence that his party would start in half an hour for the Horse Shoe. I did not feel easy until I was assured by the landlord that they had actually embarked on the Belle.

Perhaps it was useless for me to attempt to conceal the father's infirmity from the children; but I believed that the colonel's present excess was exceptional, and I hoped he would not again indulge so deeply. I could not endure the thought of witnessing the shame and mortification of Waddie and Minnie, if compelled to encounter their father in his intoxication. While I was considering this unpleasant subject, I heard my patient in the next room, the door of which I had left open, get out of the bed. I hastened into the apartment. The colonel stood holding on at the bed-post, and looked confused and lost. He glanced at me with a stare, and then a maudlin smile came upon his lips, as though the events of the day had suddenly flashed upon his mind, and he remembered where he was.

"I feel a little better of that pain, Wolf," said he; "but I haven't got quite over it."

"I am glad you feel better, sir," I replied.

"I'm better, but I am not well," he continued, grasping his coat, which I had hung on the bed-post.

He wanted his flask again. He had partially recovered from the effect of former drams, but he was not satisfied. He took the bottle from his pocket. Of course he would discover that it was empty. I hoped that his memory would not serve him in regard to the condition of the flask when he last drank from it, for I was afraid he would suspect my agency in emptying it. With some difficulty he unscrewed the stopple, and took a tumbler from the wash-stand. He turned the bottle until it was inverted over the glass, but not a drop came forth. His hands trembled, and his frame quivered. Lowering the flask from the glass, he gazed as steadily at me as his shaky condition would permit. He was angry, and I dreaded his wrath.

"Wolf, I left this flask half full of brandy," said he, fixing a stern gaze upon me. "It was very choice brandy, which my friend in Ruoara gave me for sickness."

He paused, and continued to stare at me, with a

savage frown on his brow. It was useless for me to say anything, and I did not speak.

"For sickness, Wolf," repeated he. "I told you I was sick, and I take brandy for it."

He stopped again, but I made no reply.

"Did you empty this flask, Wolf?" demanded he, sternly.

"I did, sir," I answered, as gently as I could speak.

"You did!" roared he.

"Yes, sir; I did."

He dropped into a chair, though he did not for an instant remove his gaze from me. I had no difficulty in coming to the conclusion that I had got into a bad scrape; but I had acted for the best.

"You impudent puppy!" said he, grinding his teeth.

I was silent and motionless.

"Are you my guardian?"

"I have tried to take care of you, sir."

"What do you mean by that?" he continued, after thinking a moment, probably to determine the meaning of my words.

I think he had sense enough to understand his own condition, though doubtless he did not realize how helpless he had been. The fact that I had emptied his flask assured him that I understood his situation perfectly. He knew I had helped him into the bed. It is reasonable to suppose that he was ashamed of himself, even after he had put in the plea of sickness. But for the magnate of Centreport to be thus humiliated before one whom he regarded as a dependant appeared to be more than he could endure, and the thought stirred his ire.

"I have done what I could for you, sir," I replied, evasively.

"What did you throw away my brandy — my medicine — for?"

"Because I thought you had taken enough, sir," I answered, finding that it was useless for me to attempt to dodge the issue.

"You did!"

"Yes, sir. You were very much intoxicated," I continued, mildly, but firmly.

He sprang to his feet with a celerity of which I had not believed him capable; and I began to think it would be necessary for me to run for life. He halted before me an instant, and then rushed out of the room.

CHAPTER XI.

A GENEROUS TIPPLER.

I WAS not anxious to quarrel with Colonel Wimpleton, for he carried too many guns for me; but I followed him out of the apartment, keeping at a respectful distance behind him. He went into the bar-room, and called for brandy. The landlord, who was behind the counter, pretended not to understand him, and began to speak of something else.

"Brandy!" repeated the great man, in a loud and imperative tone.

It was folly to attempt to refuse him, and the landlord promptly placed the fire-water before his savage guest. The colonel poured out and swallowed a large potion of the fiery fluid. Throwing down the payment for the dram with a lordly air, he turned and departed from the room. I stepped out of his way as he approached, concluding that my mission was finished. I decided to take the dummy back to Middleport. The colonel returned to his chamber, while I moved towards the outside door. I did not wish to have a scene with him. I had, with what now seemed to me unparalleled audacity, told him he was drunk. I expected to be discharged from my position as captain of the steamer, and to be annihilated at once.

"Wolf!" shouted he from his room.

I was not absolutely afraid of him, though I dreaded his violence. I went to the door of his apartment, and entered. He sat on the bed, and looked up at me. He did not appear to be as savage as before. The heavy dram he had just taken was beginning to have its effect, and his expression was rather maudlin and silly than stern.

"If you have no further occasion for me, I think I will return to Middleport by the dummy."

"Don't go. I want you," said he. "You said I was drunk."

"Yes, sir; I did say so; but only to explain what I had done."

"Do you mean to say I *was* drunk, Wolf?"

"Yes, sir; I have no doubt of it," I replied, with a candor which astonished myself.

"You are the first person that ever told me I was drunk."

"I hope it will be the last time any one will have occasion to say so, sir."

"Don't preach to me, Wolf. You are a very proper young man, but I never let any one preach to me. You say I *was* drunk."

"Yes, sir; and you are drunk now."

"Now?" he repeated, with a silly laugh.

"Yes, sir. You fell down between the rails this afternoon, and the train came very near backing over you. When you arrived here you couldn't possibly stand up," I answered, as honestly as though I had been his social equal.

I was amazed at my own temerity; but I had already incurred his displeasure, and with the possibility of opening his eyes to the scandal of his beastly conduct, I made up my mind that I might as well be hanged for an old sheep as a lamb, and that it should not be my fault if he did not thoroughly comprehend his disgraceful situation.

"What has become of Waddie and that girl?" he inquired.

"What girl?"

"Why, the Toppleton girl."

"They have gone to the Horse Shoe, sir; but they were in the house when you arrived."

"Were they? Why didn't you tell me of it?"

"I would not have had them see you as you were then for all you are worth."

He pursed up his lips, as he had a habit of doing when he was vexed or chagrined, and gazed upon the floor.

"You think I was drunk — do you, Wolf?"

"I know you were, sir; and I took you into this room, and put you to bed. I kept you out of sight of Waddie and Miss Minnie, and told the landlord not to tell any one you were here," I continued, with considerable spirit.

"Did you say you thought I was drunk, Wolf?" repeated he again.

"I am entirely satisfied that you were — beastly drunk," I answered, resolved, if there was any sense at all in him, that he should not misunderstand me.

"Wolf, bring me a pen and ink," he added, after gazing at the floor a while.

"Don't you think you had better lie down and take another nap, sir?"

"Bring me a pen and ink, I say."

"I think you had better lie down."

"Will you bring me a pen and ink, or shall I go myself for them?" said he, sharply.

I did not think he could use a pen if I brought one, and I could not imagine what he wished to write. I had no success in evading his requests, and I went to the office for pen and ink. I placed the articles upon the table, and wondered what was to be done. The colonel rose from his seat on the bed, and bracing up his nerves, walked tolerably straight across the floor, seating himself at the table.

"Don't you want some paper, sir?"

"No; bring me my coat," he replied.

I handed him the garment, and he took from one of the pockets of it a small, narrow book, which he opened upon the table. I was in hopes he intended to write a temperance pledge, or something of that sort. He dipped the pen in the ink, and, with a convulsive effort, began to write. I saw that the little volume before him was a pocket check-book. He wrote what I supposed to be the date, for I was not impolite enough to look over his shoulder.

"Wolf, do you say, upon your honor, that you thought I was drunk?" said he, turning around, and looking me full in the face, as though there was still a doubt upon the point.

"I know you were, sir; but if you think I am mistaken, I will call the landlord."

"Did he see me, too?"

"He couldn't well help seeing you."

"It's a mistake, Wolf. I never was drunk in my life," muttered he, in a lower tone, as he wrote in the check-book.

I could form no very accurate idea of the current of thought which was passing in his mind. The fury of his wrath had suddenly abated, though I had told him the whole truth, and nothing but the truth. I could not imagine for what purpose he was drawing a check, unless it was to pay my wages, and discharge me from his service. He wrote very rapidly, and by jerks, apparently taking advantage of momentary periods, when his nerves were more quiet. He finished the writing, after he had regularly made the memoranda in the margin to indicate the amount and the payee of the check. It was marvellous to me that he could write at all, and especially so that he was able to go through all the business forms so correctly. He tore the check from the book, and with a very peculiar smile on his face, thrust it out at arm's length towards me.

"Take that, Wolf," said he, the drunken leer on his face becoming more intense.

"What is it, sir?"

"Take it."

I obeyed him. It was a check for ten thousand dollars, payable to Wolf Penniman or bearer. I was astonished and bewildered.

"What is this for, sir?" I inquired.

"You can draw the money at the Centreport Bank," he replied.

"I do not understand you, Colonel Wimpleton."

"I make you a present of ten thousand dollars, Wolf; can't you understand that?" said he, the leer on his face deepening to a laugh.

"What is it for, sir?"

"That's what I owe you, Wolf."

"I think not."

"O, I do," protested he, vehemently; "you saved my life once, but I never gave you a dollar for it."

"But you gave me the command of the steamer, sir."

"No matter for that. You beat the Lake Shore Line in her, and put twice that sum of money into my pocket by it. The money is yours, Wolf. Now don't say another word about it."

What was the magnate thinking about? What had given him this sudden fit of generosity? A few moments before, he had been angry with me; now he had gone to the other extreme. But the man was intoxicated. I did not regard the check as mine, for it was the gift of a man not in his right mind. It was a princely sum for a young person in my situation; but the thought that the money would ever come into my possession did not occur to me.

"Now, Wolf, you are my friend," said he. "If you think I'm drunk, a friend must bear a friend's infirmities — humor them, and try to hide them. Do you understand me, Wolf?"

"Is this the price of my silence in regard to the

events of to-day?" I asked, beginning to think that this was the solution of his extraordinary generosity.

"No, no; by no means!" protested he. "It's only just what I ought to do for all you have done for me, and for Waddie."

"But I cannot take this, sir. Your secret, so far as it is a secret, is safe in my keeping. I have prevented you from being seen by Waddie and Minnie."

"I say, Wolf, you shall keep it," he replied, with an oath, as he brought his fist down upon the table with such force as to make the ink fly from the inkstand.

It was useless to contend, and I did not attempt to oppose him.

"I would rather have your name to another paper than to this one," I replied, rather jocosely, as I laid the check upon the table, and pointed to it with my finger.

"What's that, Wolf?" he demanded, with excited interest. "Bring the paper. Let me see it."

I took the blank sheet of a letter from my pocket, and wrote as follows: "I promise, on the honor of a man and a gentleman, to abstain entirely from the use of intoxicating drinks, unless prescribed by a physician." I pushed the paper across the table to him. Adjusting his eye-glass, he read it.

"I would rather have your name to that paper than to this," I repeated, pointing to the check, and pushing it towards him.

"Do you mean to insult me, Wolf?" demanded he, sternly.

"By no means, sir," I replied, fearful that I had gone too far. "I mean exactly what I say."

Taking the paper from the table, he indignantly tore it into very small pieces, and then, rushing to the window, threw them out.

"I am not an idiot! I am not a child!" protested he. "I know what I am about, you see."

"I did not mean to offend you, sir."

"You have the check. We will change the subject," he added, with an attempt to put on his dignity. "I am not offended. Now, where is Waddie?"

"On the Horse Shoe, I suppose, unless he has left for home."

"Is the Toppleton girl with him?"

"I believe she is."

"Courting!" sneered he. "I won't have it! No, I won't!"

"I assure you, sir, that you are entirely mistaken. I have seen Tom Walton, who has been with them all day, and he says Waddie behaves like a gentleman to Miss Toppleton, and nothing more."

"But they are together."

"You have nothing to fear from Waddie, if they are."

"I am going over to the Horse Shoe, Wolf. I'm going to stop this thing before it goes any farther," said he, rising, and putting on his coat.

"I hope you will not, sir," I interposed.

"I will."

"I cannot keep your secret, if you expose yourself."

"I am as regular as you are, Wolf;" and he went out of the room by the door opening into the entry.

I followed him, determined that he should not go to the Horse Shoe, if I could possibly prevent him from doing so.

CHAPTER XII.

ANOTHER CALAMITY.

IT was not easy to prevent a man like Colonel Wimpleton from having his own way. He was not nearly so bad as he had been before he went to bed; but he was still in no condition to exhibit himself to his son and daughter. He went to the landlord and paid the bill. He then produced his flask, and demanded that it should be filled. The hotel-keeper demurred, and did not sell liquor except by the glass; but the colonel began to storm and swear, and he was obliged to comply.

Just then I happened to think that I had left the check the colonel had given me on the table, in the room he had occupied, and I hastened to get it; for, though I did not mean to use it myself, I did not intend that any one else should do so. It was not where I had left it, or where I supposed I had left it.

It was not on the table, and it was not on the floor. In a word, I could not find it, though I made a diligent search in every part of the room, thinking the wind might have blown it from the table. The door of the adjoining room, where I had remained a portion of the time, was open, and I passed through this apartment into the entry.

I searched my pockets, thinking I might possibly have deposited it in one of them, while I was talking with the colonel. The last time I remembered to have noticed it, was when I pointed to it, after the tipsy great man had read the paper I wrote. Then the conversation became rather exciting to me, and I walked across the room several times. It was possible that the colonel had torn up both the check and the pledge at the same time.

"Where are you, Wolf? I'm looking for you," said the colonel, appearing at the entry door.

"Did you tear up the check you wrote, sir?"

"The check?" repeated he, evidently trying to stimulate his memory.

"You wrote a check for ten thousand dollars in my favor, and handed it to me."

"Yes, of course; I know that," replied he, impatiently, as though my statement implied that he had not known what he was about when he did the generous act. "I was trying to think whether I tore it up with the other paper. I didn't mean to tear it up; and if I did, I will give you another."

"I cannot find it anywhere," I added.

"Then, of course, I destroyed it with the other paper. I will give you another just like it," said he, dropping into the chair before the table.

"I would not write another now, sir," I interposed. "Perhaps I may find the other, or at least the pieces of it, if you tore it up."

I did not regard the check as of any consequence to me, under the circumstances; but it was possible, if it fell into the hands of some other person, that an improper use might be made of it; and for this reason only was I anxious to ascertain what had become of it. I left the colonel sitting at the table, and went out doors to see if I could find any of the pieces of the check. The window, from which he had thrown the fragments of paper, opened into an alley between the hotel and the adjoining building, through which the wind blew quite sharply. I could not find even a single piece of either paper; but I continued the search at the leeward of the hotel. I found two or three pieces of the paper I had written, on the railroad; but the rest of them had probably gone into the lake. I was no wiser than before; but I was forced to conclude that, as I could not find the check, the colonel must have destroyed it with the other paper. Both of them had lain on the table, within his reach, for I remembered that I had pushed the check towards him, when I told him I would rather have his name on the pledge I had written. If the valuable little paper was destroyed, it was all right, and I need trouble myself no more about it.

"Hallo, Wolf."

I turned. It was Nick Van Wolter.

"How are you, Nick?" I replied.

"What are you looking for, Wolf?"

I did not deem it necessary to inform him what I was looking for; so I did not give him a direct answer.

"Where is the colonel? I heard he was on a regular bat!" asked Nick, with a coarse grin.

"He is at the hotel."

"The landlord told me he was there," continued Nick. "You see, I was mixed up in this business down here this morning. After the Raven upset, Waddie sent me home in her. I got to Centreport just as the steamer was going out, and I went on board of her, and came down as far as Ruoara. My father told me that the colonel was on a regular bat,"—by which I understood him to mean a spree. "He said you had crossed the lake with him, and that something was said about going to Grass Springs. I was a little curious to know what was going on, as I was with the party this morning."

I could not exactly see why Nick had volunteered this explanation.

"Did you think the colonel was after the party?" I inquired.

"From what my father said, I supposed he was."

Then the mate had understood Colonel Wimpleton much better than I could, before we left the Ucayga, which seemed a little odd to me.

"What did your father say?" I asked.

"He said the colonel was on a regular bat, and

that he was mad. I knew the fellows and girls went off together, and I concluded the colonel had found it out, and that was what made him mad. I didn't want to have Waddie get into any scrape with his father when he was a little over the bay; for you know the colonel isn't exactly a saint when he is all right, and I suppose he isn't any better when he is tight. So I took a boat at Ruoara, and sailed over this way. I saw the party on the island, though I didn't go very near it, for I didn't want them to see me, unless it was necessary. I saw the colonel was not there; so I came over here, and found he was at the hotel. I thought, if there was any danger of his going over to the Horse Shoe, I would see Waddie in season to tip him the wink. You understand me, Wolf?"

"Yes, I understand."

"You see, if the colonel caught Waddie and Miss Minnie with Tom and his sister, he would raise Cain with them."

"I do not think that he would trouble them under ordinary circumstances," I replied.

"O, yes, he would!" protested Nick, who, strangely

enough, as I thought, seemed to know more about the matter than I did.

"Certainly he suspects some mischief to-day, though I do not understand why he should. He insists upon going over to the Horse Shoe, Nick; and I don't know that I can prevent him from doing so. You have a boat here?"

"Yes; the one I hired at Ruoara."

"If you will go over to the Horse Shoe, as you return, and give them a hint that Colonel Wimpleton is after them, I will be very much obliged to you."

"O, I will do that, certainly," replied the obliging Nick.

"Don't say a word about his being out of the way."

"No; certainly not," answered he, with a prudent shake of the head.

"You understand the case as well as I do, and you must manage it as best you can."

"I'll go right over;" and he hastened towards the landing, which was a short distance up the lake.

I returned to the hotel, abundantly satisfied with the arrangement I had made. While I could not exactly understand how Nick happened so accurately to divine the object of the colonel's visit to the Springs, I was willing to admit that it was very kind of him to endeavor to save Waddie and Minnie from the wrath of their tipsy father. I found the colonel still seated at the table, though I was soon convinced that he had not been there all the time of my absence; for his limbs were more unsteady, and his voice thicker, than when I had left him. He had evidently taken another dram.

"There's another check, Wolf," said he, handing me a duplicate of the former one, which, I noticed, was regularly numbered, as the first had been.

"I didn't mean to destroy the other."

"Perhaps you did not, sir; though I cannot find it."

"No matter; put the check in your pocket. Now take me over to the Horse Shoe, and I will put an end to this courting business."

"I think it is rather late to go there to-night; and it looks a little like another shower," I replied.

"Don't talk to me, Wolf! I say I'm going to the Horse Shoe."

It was useless to contend, and I accompanied him down to the public landing. As I had sent Nick forward to warn the party of the approach of the colonel, I was satisfied there would be no scene that day. The only boat I could obtain at the landing was a small bateau, very frail and unsteady for such a burden as I had to carry. I objected to using it, but Colonel Wimpleton declared it would do very well, and insisted that I should row him over to the island. I deemed it dangerous to do so, and I tried to deter him; but he was as obstinate as usual, and all the more obstinate for being intoxicated. Very reluctantly I helped him into the bateau, and soon repented that I had not absolutely refused to go with him.

While I was getting ready, I had occasion to regret that his flask had been refilled, for he took a long draught from it. When he had with great difficulty taken his seat in the stern of the boat, I pushed off. I saw nothing of the Belle, though the boat in which Nick had come from Ruoara lay on the shore of the island, where he had landed to communicate with the party. Another shower was coming up from the south-west, and I thought our chances for getting a ducking were very good. The last dram of my passenger had begun to produce its effect, and he swayed to and fro on his unsteady seat, and I regretted very much that I had consented to come with him.

When I had pulled about two thirds of the distance to the Horse Shoe, I saw the Belle standing out from the deep channel, on the other side of the island. Nick had delivered his message, and the peril of a disagreeable encounter was avoided. I called the attention of the colonel to the fact that the party had left the Horse Shoe, hoping he would permit me to row back to Grass Springs. Unfortunately, the intelligence produced a different effect upon him, and roused his anger.

"Stop zem, Wolf! Stop zem!" said he, angrily.

I did hail the Belle, but no notice was taken of my call.

"Pull for zat boat," added he, pointing to the Belle.

He did not know what he was about, and I decided not to heed his requests. Nick had now embarked in his sail-boat, and in order to double the southern part of the island, was obliged to stand out towards my craft.

"Why don't you do dzi tell you, Wolf?" demanded the colonel, rising in the boat as though he intended to come at me.

His legs yielded beneath him, and he dropped upon the rail of the bateau, careening the frail skiff till the water poured in over the side. Before I could get hold of him, he rolled over into the lake. I was horror-struck, for it was no easy matter to rescue a heavy man, as tipsy as he was.

CHAPTER XIII.

AFTER THE ACCIDENT.

MY skiff was nearly full of water, which rendered it quite unmanageable. In my attempt to save Colonel Wimpleton before he went into the water, I had lost both oars overboard. There was no romance in leaping into the lake after a tipsy man, and there were two chances that he would drown me to one that I should save him. I did not consider such a movement on my part as hopeful, and therefore I did not make it. I simply endeavored to recover my oars, and back the boat so that the struggling magnate could get hold of it.

The colonel floundered and fought the destroying element with mad zeal; but of course the more he labored the worse it was for him. It was evident that he could not hold out long, and what was done must be quickly done, or it would be too late.

One of my oars floated on the water not six feet from me, but I could not move the boat, for the want of anything like a paddle. I coiled up the painter, and threw it so that the end dropped beyond the oar. I pulled in, but the line slipped over it. I then tied a heavy bunch of keys I had in my pocket to the end of the painter, and tried again. This effort was successful, and I hauled in the oar till I could reach it with my hand.

I placed it in the stern, heaved the skiff round, and sculled with all my might towards the drowning magnate; but the boat rolled, and dipped the water over her gunwale, so that I made little or no progress. My heart was in my mouth, and I was almost certain the colonel would drown, when Nick Van Wolter's boat dashed by me. The helm was put hard down, and, as the craft came up into the wind, Nick sprang into the bow. He certainly managed the matter exceedingly well, whatever bungling he had done earlier in the day. Reaching down, he seized the drowning magnate by the collar of his coat with both hands, and held on with all his might.

If Colonel Wimpleton had been sober, he would not have fallen into the water; but if he had fallen overboard being sober, and had remained in the water so long, he would certainly have been drowned, for drunken men seem to have a remarkable facility for escaping from perils which overwhelm men in their right mind. Nick held on to his helpless burden like a good fellow, and I struggled to urge forward my water-logged boat, so as to render him some assistance. The skiff and the oars had drifted some distance from the spot, and my efforts were absolutely vain.

"Hurry up, Wolf!" shouted Nick, with a gasp, extorted from him by the weight of his burden.

"My skiff is full of water, and I can't do anything with it," I replied.

Taking the oar from the stern, I tried to paddle the skiff. I succeeded better, but my progress was very slow. I saw Nick make a tremendous effort to haul in the colonel. He stood upon the gunwale of the boat, and as he lifted with all his strength, the craft careened, and he dragged the shoulders of his burden up to the rail. Falling back himself as he gained in his task, the boat righted a little, and assisted in lifting the heavy load. After pausing a moment to recover his breath, he renewed the effort, and, to my great satisfaction, he hauled the colonel into the boat, just as I came within a painter's length of him.

"Catch this rope, Nick," I called to him, as I coiled up my painter, ready to toss it to him.

But Nick had sunk down upon the thwart, overcome by the violence of his efforts. So I paddled away again with the oar, and at last came alongside the sail-boat. I jumped aboard, and hastened to ascertain the condition of the colonel. It seemed to me he must be filled with water; but perhaps the natural repulsion of the pure element for the viler one with which he was thoroughly saturated, saved him. Of course the severe ordeal to which he had been subjected nullified the effects of the brandy he had drank. Nick had placed him upon a seat, but he was unable to sit up. He had not lost his senses, strange as it may seem; but he was completely exhausted by the violence of his struggles.

"How do you feel, Colonel Wimpleton?" I asked.

He made me no reply, though he looked up at me. I took my handkerchief, wiped his face and head, and rubbed his temples. He began to shiver with the chill of his cold bath, and to throw up the water he had swallowed. He was rather stupid, and did not answer any of the questions I put to him. By this time Nick had recovered in a measure from his exhaustion, and wanted to do something more for the comfort of the great man he had saved.

"What shall we do, Wolf?" asked he.

"Run for Grass Springs," I replied.

He hauled in the sheet, and put the helm up, heading the boat to the point I suggested.

"That was a narrow escape for the colonel," added Nick, in a low tone, as he glanced at the sufferer on the seat.

"Yes, it was. You came just at the right time. My skiff was full of water, and I could not get along. I lost my oars when the colonel went over."

"How did it happen?"

I shook my head slightly, to indicate that we had better not discuss this matter in the presence of the colonel. Seeing that the skiff, whose painter I had made fast to the sail-boat, retarded her progress, I cast it off, and let it go adrift. There was a fair breeze, and the craft made good time through the water; but nearly half an hour must elapse before we could reach Grass Springs, which was about two miles distant. I placed myself by the side of the colonel, and began to rub him again; but a gesture of impatience indicated that he disliked the operation, and I desisted. But I had the satisfaction of seeing that he was steadily improving. He had a fit of coughing, during which he relieved himself of much of the water he had swallowed during his struggles.

"How do you feel, colonel?" I inquired, when he had recovered from the fit.

"A little better," he replied, raising his hand to his breast pocket.

He took out his brandy flask, and attempted to remove the stopple; but his trembling hands refused to perform the task.

"Let me open it for you," I interposed.

If brandy is ever good for anything, it is for a

person in his condition. At first he was not disposed to let me take the flask.

"I think you need a little now. It will do you good," I added.

Then he permitted me to take the bottle, and I unscrewed the top. Pouring a quantity of it into the cup, which formed the lower part of the flask, I offered it to him. He looked into it, and held it out to me.

"Put more in," said he.

I obeyed him, and filled the cup nearly full.

"Will you have some water with it?" I inquired.

"No;" and he drank it off, or rather poured it down his throat.

I have no doubt it warmed his stomach, and afforded him immediate relief from the intense chill which pervaded his frame. At any rate, he ceased to shiver. Before we reached the shore, he took another, but smaller dose, and then declared that he was quite comfortable.

By this time the Belle was off Ruoara, and I concluded that those on board of her were in happy ignorance of the alarming event which had just transpired. When I had first seen her, she was beating towards home, and at the time of the accident she had run behind the southern point of the Horse Shoe. It was very fortunate that we had not been seen, for Waddie and his sister were again spared the pain and mortification of beholding their father in the most pitiable condition to which a man can be reduced.

As soon as we landed I procured a carriage, and we conveyed the colonel to the hotel. The landlord provided dry clothing for him, and we rubbed his limbs with flannel till the circulation was restored. He continued to drink brandy, but it did not seem to have so powerful an effect upon him as before his involuntary bath. Though he did not say anything about the exciting event of the day, I have no doubt he kept up a tremendous thinking. In the evening, after his clothes had been dried, and he had eaten his supper, he said he wanted to go home. He consented, at Nick's suggestion, to go to Ruoara in the boat in which the latter had come from that place, and we embarked just after dark. We borrowed a heavy overcoat for him, and he kept warm on the passage, which, in the fresh breeze we had, was made in an hour and a quarter.

At Ruoara I procured a carriage and a pair of fast horses; but it was eleven o'clock when we reached the colonel's mansion in Centreport. He invited us to go in on our arrival, and led the way to the library. His family had all retired, for he was frequently away nights, and they had learned not to sit up for him.

"I suppose all this will be in the newspapers by to-morrow, or next day," said the colonel, as he seated himself before the fire he had ordered John, his man, to make.

"No, sir, not at all!" protested Nick. "We didn't even tell the landlord over to the hotel at Grass Springs what had happened to you — did we, Wolf?"

"We did not. I am not aware that any one except ourselves knows anything about it," I replied.

"And no one ever shall," added Nick, looking at me, and evidently speaking for both of us.

"Certainly not," I answered. "If there is nothing more that I can do for you to-night, Colonel Wimpleton, I believe I will go home."

"You can sleep here, Wolf," suggested the colonel.

"I thank you, sir; but I think I will go home," I replied; and, bidding him good night, I left the house.

I had a skiff at the wharf, in which I pulled across the lake. It was after midnight when I reached my father's house. My mother let me in, and of course she wanted to know where I had been. I simply replied that I had been to Grass Springs with Colonel Wimpleton, evading all her inquiries in regard to the object of the visit. I went to my room immediately. When I put my hand in my vest pocket for the key of my watch, which it was my custom to wind on retiring, I felt the duplicate check which my employer had given me. I took it out, and unfolded it. The paper was written in due form, and I had no doubt it was good for the ten thousand dollars for which it was drawn.

The check had been given me by an intoxicated man. It was not possible that he would have done so absurd a thing if he had been sober. Certainly it was not morally right for me to take advantage of his great infirmity. Though the donor could give me this large sum, and not feel the loss, yet it seemed to be nothing less than robbery to use the check. It would be base and dishonorable in me to hold him to a promise given in his inebriation. I might lose the check if I kept it, and another might find it who had less scruples. If I left it at home, my father and mother might discover it, and desire an explanation, which I could not give.

Rather impulsively, I folded up the check, lighted it at the lamp, and threw it into the fireplace. I watched the paper till it was entirely consumed, and then scattered and ground up with my foot the tinder which was left. Having thus prevented the check from doing any mischief in the future, I went to bed.

CHAPTER XIV.

"THE OCCURRENCES OF YESTERDAY."

THE next morning, at eight o'clock, my father and I crossed the lake to perform our daily duties on board of the steamer, which arrived from Hitaca at half past eight. I could not help thinking of the stirring events of the previous day, and I was anxious to learn whether the colonel had suffered any serious injury in consequence of his bath, and more especially in consequence of the inordinate quantity of brandy he had drank. While I was waiting for the arrival of the Ucayga, Waddie came down the wharf, and, as he walked with a brisk step directly towards me, I had no doubt his mission there was with me.

"How are you this morning, Wolf?" said he.

"All right. How is it with you, after the disaster of yesterday?" I inquired.

"I'm all right, except my shoulder, which don't feel quite so well to-day. My mother thinks I took a little cold in it."

"How is your sister? I hope she don't suffer any on account of her bath."

"O, no! She is as bright as a dollar this morning. By the great horn spoon, it was a close shave she made of it! Tom Walton may say what he pleases, but I believe, if Tommy Toppleton hadn't swam after her, she would have been drowned, for she says she was sinking when he got hold of her."

"You must have a safer boat, Waddie, if your sister is going to sail with you," I added. "I didn't quite like the looks of the craft the other day, when I saw her."

"The Raven is safe enough. She may be a little crank, but she can outsail anything on the lake. It wasn't her fault that she upset yesterday. Any boat would have gone over treated as she was;" and he proceeded to explain the circumstances implicating Nick Van Wolter, which have already been stated.

"Now, what was the matter with my father yesterday, Wolf?" asked Waddie; but he looked so good-natured about it that I was sure he did not suspect the mortifying truth. "You went up to Grass Springs with him, in search of our party."

"I did. Your father suspected that you and Grace, and Tommy and Miss Wimpleton, were becoming too well acquainted."

"Grace and I!" laughed Waddie, opening his eyes. "You can tell him from me that there isn't a particle of truth in that."

His earnest declaration removed the last doubt that disturbed me.

"I don't know where he obtained his information, if he did obtain any, but he was very much incensed against you."

"Perhaps there will be a regular breeze one of these days, for I think myself that Tommy and Minnie like each other pretty well," added Waddie, lightly. "That's their business, not mine. Of course, I don't mean to say that anything will come of it; but I shouldn't be surprised if it did amount to something."

"Have you seen your father this morning?" I inquired, with more interest than I was willing to manifest.

"No; he had not got up when I left the house. I expect he will talk to me very seriously about yesterday; but I shall only answer for myself."

"There is not much to say," I replied.

"When he gets at the fact, as I understand it, I'm afraid poor Minnie will have to take it; but we won't borrow any trouble. I must go to school now. Of course you won't tell him what I say about Tom and Minnie."

"Certainly not."

He left me. I wanted to ask him several questions in relation to his father; but I was fearful of exposing the colonel, or awakening the curiosity of the son. It was plain enough that he had no idea of what a debauch his father had been on the day before. Those who had heard of the great man's narrow escape on the railroad were considerate enough not to mention it in Waddie's presence. I had not time to call upon the colonel, even if it had been proper for me to do so, at this early hour in the morning. The Ucayga was coming in sight from behind the Gulfport Point.

"Captain Penniman, Colonel Wimpleton told me to deliver this note to you before you left," said the magnate's man servant, handing me the epistle.

I took it, and saw that it was directed in the well-known handwriting of the colonel. He seldom wrote notes to me, and this one, after the events which had transpired the day before, excited my curiosity and interest. I tore open the envelope, and, as I read its contents, my heart rose into my throat. Before I had finished it, I made up my mind that if I had ever supposed I understood the character of Colonel Wimpleton, I was entirely mistaken. The letter was as follows:—

"WOLF PENNIMAN: After the occurrences of yesterday, I can no longer retain you in my employ as the master of the steamboat. It is not necessary to explain any further than to say that I feel compelled to discharge you from your place. You need not trouble yourself to call upon me, for I shall not see you; and henceforward you will regard me as a stranger, as I shall regard you.

"Your father may still retain his place as engineer.

He is a faithful man, and I hope he will remain where he is.

"If you have that high sense of honor for which people give you credit, you will still regard what passed between us yesterday as confidential, especially after the consideration I gave you, and which, I will add, shall not be dishonored.

WIMPLETON."

I will not say I was stunned or overwhelmed by the contents of this letter; but I was astounded. It was incomprehensible to me. I could not understand it. I had left the colonel just before midnight, and we were then apparently on as good terms as ever. He had expressed no dissatisfaction at anything I had done. I read the note a second and a third time; but it still afforded me no intimation of what wicked thing I had done to deserve such harsh treatment.

"What have you there, Wolf?" asked my father, who stood near me.

"A letter from Colonel Wimpleton," I replied, handing it to him.

He read it, and was more astounded even than I had been. I had been regarded as a necessity to the magnate of Centreport; but now I was discharged without a word of explanation, with the assurance beforehand that he would not even see me.

"Why, what does this mean, Wolf?" demanded my father; and I think I never saw him look more anxious and disturbed in my life.

"You know as much about it as I do, father," I replied.

"No, I don't. I can't tell what he means by the occurrences of yesterday."

"They had nothing whatever to do with the steamer."

"Wolf, there is some terrible secret under this."

"Indeed there is not, father," I protested. "I have done nothing which I should be ashamed to have published in the newspapers."

"I don't say that you have," answered my father, as the Ucayga came up to the wharf, and made fast. "I must know more about this."

"There are certain occurrences which I cannot mention to any one; but I think of nothing to explain this note. When I left Colonel Wimpleton's house, at nearly midnight, we were as good friends as ever. I have no idea why I am discharged."

"I'm not satisfied, Wolf."

"Neither am I; but the colonel informs me that he will give no explanation, and I suppose I may as well make the best of it."

"I want to talk with you. Can't you go down to Ucayga in the boat?"

"I have no objection, if the colonel has not."

I saw the same servant who had delivered the note to me hasten on board the Ucayga as soon as the plank was laid down. He had a letter in his hand, which I saw him give to Van Wolter. As soon as the passengers landed I went on board of the boat. The first person I met was the mate.

"What's going on, Captain Penniman?" said he, in high excitement.

"I only know that I am dismissed," I answered.

"Read that," he added, handing me his letter.

It simply informed him that he was appointed captain of the steamer, at the same salary I had received, and that he would enter upon the discharge of his duties immediately.

"What's the trouble, Captain Penniman?" asked he, as I returned the letter.

"I haven't the least idea, Captain Van Wolter," I replied; and by this time I had fully recovered my self-possession.

"This is all new to me. I never asked to be appointed captain of this boat, and never expected the place," he continued.

"I am satisfied you did not. I congratulate you upon your promotion, with all my heart; and I hope you will retain the place longer than I did."

"I thank you, captain; but I don't feel just right about it," said he; and really he did not seem to be half so much elated at his good fortune as I should have been. "You have always been a good friend of mine, and I don't exactly like to step into your boots in this manner."

"Don't be at all concerned about that. The colonel has his whims, and I suppose he can afford to have them, whoever suffers thereby. Take the place, and do your duty in the future, as you have in the past."

"You are very kind, Captain Penniman. Of

course I should like the place; but I don't wish to have you shoved out of it. I am tempted to decline it."

"Don't do that."

"I'm not sure that I can take the boat through the Horse Shoe Channel. You know I never tried it. Yesterday afternoon I went around the South Shoe, and came within half a minute of losing the trains."

"I will go down with you on this trip, and give you the bearings," I replied.

"You are a Christian, Wolf, if there ever was one. It is time to be off, and we will talk over the matter on the way down."

While he was starting the boat I went into the state-room, — no longer mine, — and seated myself to think over the mighty event of the hour. Why had the colonel discharged me? I had told him the plain truth in regard to his condition. I had spoken to him as directly as Nathan did to David when he said, "Thou art the man." I had declared to him, in so many words, that he was drunk. Perhaps the remembrance of my plain speech was too humiliating when he was sober. It was possible that he thought I was assuming too much. As I recalled his words and his actions, his efforts to disguise his condition, and his ridiculous attempt to purchase my silence, I concluded that I had solved the problem.

No doubt the colonel was ashamed of himself, and he could not endure the reflection that any human being, and especially one whom he regarded as his dependant, had dared to tell him he was intoxicated. The note indicated wounded pride in its tone. I was willing to accept this explanation, for I could think of no other. The colonel was certainly considerate towards my father; and this favor, with the check, which he took pains to say would not be dishonored, was doubtless deemed sufficient to conciliate me, and keep me from exposing the secrets of the chamber at the hotel in Grass Springs. The note was mild in its terms; and perhaps the writer thought that, with ten thousand dollars in my pocket, I should not take a place on the railroad line.

While I was thinking of the matter, my father, who had asked Christy Holgate to take charge of the engine on his down trip, came into the room, and seated himself before me. He was very much agitated; and the fact that he had not been discharged did not close his eyes to the vast injustice which had been done to me. He wanted the matter settled at once, and he would not run the engine another day if I could not have fair play. I begged him to keep cool, and he began to question me very sharply in regard to the "occurrences of yesterday."

CHAPTER XV.

A TEMPTING OFFER.

"WOLF, there is a story in circulation that Colonel Wimpleton was very much intoxicated yesterday," said my father, as he seated himself in the state-room. "I heard two passengers speaking of it on the main deck, just now. Is this one of the occurrences of yesterday?"

"Probably Colonel Wimpleton does not so regard it," I replied.

"They say he fell off the train, and came very near being killed."

"That is not true. He got out of the car when the train stopped to avoid killing a cow. It started before he could get on. When I missed him, I induced the conductor to go back, for I was afraid he had been hurt. He was on the track, and came very near being run over; but he did not fall off.

We put on the brakes hard, or he might have been killed," I added, stating the case as mildly as possible.

"If he don't brake up there will an end of him," said my father, shaking his head. "They say he drinks very hard."

"I think there is no doubt about that."

"You picked him up, I suppose," continued my father.

"I assisted in doing it. Of course all this was known to the people on the train."

"It's no secret, for the passengers on board are spreading it as fast as they can. But what else happened yesterday?"

"Colonel Wimpleton regards these matters as confidential, and I do not consider myself at liberty to speak of them. I can only say I did nothing to compromise myself, and, except getting intoxicated, I don't know that the colonel did. There is really no secret to be revealed; and I don't think the colonel wishes to conceal anything, except the fact that he was intoxicated."

"But everybody knows that.

"Everybody but the tippler himself," I added.

"He thinks no one has any idea that he drinks more than he can carry."

"You took care of him while he was in this state."

"I did what I could for him."

"And he discharges you for this!" exclaimed my father, compressing his lips, as if to suppress his indignation.

"Colonel Wimpleton occupies a high position. He is a very proud man. As I understand the matter, he does not want any one in his employ who has witnessed his degradation and humiliation. That is all I can make of it. As I said before, I have no idea of the reason why I am discharged."

"It's very singular," added my father, with a puzzled expression.

We continued to discuss the subject, with no better results, till I was called to pilot the boat through the Horse Shoe Channel. I gave all the bearings to Captain Van Wolter, but he declared it was the most difficult piece of navigation he knew of, and he did not believe his nerves would ever let him do it. I regarded it as a very easy matter, because I had learned every foot of the bottom in my small boat. After the Ucayga passed into the open lake again, Van Wolter came into the state-room, where my father still remained. We again debated the knotty problem, and the new captain was fair and square in his position. If my father had any suspicion that he had used underhand means to obtain the place, I had none.

When the Ucayga returned to Centreport, all of us had become tolerably reconciled to the new order of things. I advised my father to attend to his duty as usual, and say nothing about me. Hard as it was for him, he consented, and I went on shore, taking with me all my effects, and bidding good by to my associates. My occupation was gone; but it was not generally known yet that I had been superseded. I was not disposed to make any sensation; so I took my skiff and pulled over to Middleport. I went home, and had a three hours' talk with my mother upon "the occurrences of yesterday," so far as I felt justified in alluding to them. Then I went out into the garden, which my father and I were planting in our leisure hours.

I had plenty of time for reflection. I was out of

employment now; but I had saved my wages, and did not feel much concerned about the future, though I had no idea of remaining long without work. Captain Portman, who had come after me the year before to serve as skipper of his yacht, might still wish to employ me in that capacity. Very likely Major Toppleton would give me a position as soon as he learned that his great rival had dismissed me. The Belle was still my property; but I could not think of depriving my good friend Tom Walton of the excellent business he was doing in her. He paid me a very handsome income on my investment in the boat. While I was thus meditating upon the past and the future, I saw Waddie Wimpleton coming up the walk towards me. He had heard 'the news.

"Wolf, I shall not stand this. By the great horn spoon, I shall not," said he, in excited tones, as he grasped my dirty hand, with which I had been dropping potatoes.

"What's the matter, Waddie?" I asked, pleasantly and coolly.

"I am the president of the Steamboat Company, and until I discharge you, you are not discharged."

"I am willing to waive the forms."

"I don't care for the forms. You are still captain of the steamer."

"Have you seen your father?"

"I have; he is not very well to-day."

I did not see how he could be very well after the debauch of the day before.

"What does he say?" I asked.

"He will not say anything that satisfies me. He don't want you any longer, and he says you are entirely satisfied with what he has done. Is that so?"

"I can't say that it is. I do not understand why I am discharged. Here is your father's note to me," I added, handing him the letter.

He read it, and looked even more puzzled than before.

"Well, what does all this mean? 'Occurrences of yesterday,' 'confidential,' 'consideration,'" he added, glancing over the note a second time.

"So far as there was anything confidential between your father and me, it must remain so."

"Of course," said Waddie. "I don't mean to pry into anything that does not concern me."

"Now, Waddie, I am going to submit to the action of your father, and I wish you to do the same."

"I can't do it," protested he. "It is mean to discharge you in this manner."

"Not as your father understands it," I replied, thinking of the ten thousand dollars he had given me, perhaps intended, at the time it was given, to compensate me for being discharged.

"If I am not to be allowed to know the facts, of course I can't judge whether it is mean or not."

"I advise you not to mention the matter to any one. There is something unpleasant about the occurrences of yesterday, and the more you stir the subject, the more unpleasant it will become."

Waddie looked at me, and a certain sadness which overspread his face assured me that he was not ignorant of his father's infirmity. He was not disposed to talk with me about it, or to acknowledge the terrible truth.

"Wolf, we all have a theory to explain everything; and I have mine," said he, after a long pause. "I am afraid you have got into this scrape by what you did for our party yesterday. My father believes that Tommy Toppleton is in love with Minnie, or I with Grace. He hates the Toppletons as badly as ever, and I am afraid he would rather see us dead than have a marriage between the two families."

"Does he say anything?"

"Not a word; it isn't his style. If he caught us together he would. He spoke of going to Europe this morning for his health, and of taking Minnie and me with him. He is thinking how he can separate us from the Toppletons. From his taking you with him yesterday, he must have supposed you knew what was going on."

"Why should he suppose so?" I asked.

"I don't know. Then you sent Nick Van Wolter to warn us to keep out of the way."

"He could not have known that."

"Perhaps he did."

"How?"

"I have about come to the conclusion that Nick is a snake."

"Do you think so?" I added, rather startled by the suggestion.

"John says Nick did not leave my father till after one o'clock last night; and I know he was in the library to-day."

"What makes you think Nick is a snake?"

"I don't like his actions. He is a regular swell, to begin with. I am not sure of anything, but I can't help thinking that Nick told my father you sent him to warn us to keep out of his way. If he knew that he would not look at you again as long as he lives."

"It may be so."

"I shall keep an eye on Nick, and find out, if possible, what is going on between him and my father."

"I hope Nick is not playing foul," I added, musing.

"I shall follow your advice, Wolf, and keep still for a while; but I am not going to let this thing rest as it is a great while. My father told me to pay you your last week's salary. Here is a check for the amount."

I took the check, for I had fairly earned the money. Waddie was determined to know more, and only his fear of opening a tender subject prevented him from taking a stand at once in my favor. He left me, and

I continued to plant potatoes till night I had a feeling that justice would be done me in the end, and that I could afford to wait. I determined to keep quiet for a few days, and the result of this decision was, that a great deal of work was done in our garden. But it was soon known that I had been discharged, or had voluntarily retired, from the command of the steamer. Many of my friends came to see me. Tom Walton was ready to give up the Belle; but I told him I was satisfied with the present arrangement, and would sell him the boat for whatever she would bring at auction. Tommy Toppleton, at the suggestion of his father, offered me the position of agent of the Lake Shore Railroad and Steamboat Line, at the same salary I had been receiving in the Ucayga.

This was a tempting offer; but I felt that I could do nothing for the line, and I reserved my answer for a future time. I could not suggest any plan which would enable the line to compete with the steamer, and I did not wish to increase the ill feeling between the two great men. I told Waddie of the offer made me, and he was reasonable enough to think I ought to accept it. After his father had discharged me, he had no further claims upon me. I asked him to mention the subject to his father as a "feeler," and he promised to do so. Colonel Wimpleton believed he had given me ten thousand dollars, and probably regarded this sum as a retainer against the enemy, if nothing more.

A few days after my dismissal, I went over to Centreport to draw the check given me for my last week's pay. As I walked up from the wharf, I met Colonel Wimpleton in his buggy. He glanced at me, and then looked the other way, true to his promise to treat me as a stranger. I obeyed his injunction, and did not presume to bow or otherwise recognize him. I met Nick Van Wolter, who only nodded to me, and hurried on as though he did not wish to speak with me. I could not help thinking of what Waddie had said of him, and his impression of Nick's double dealing seemed to be confirmed by his present conduct.

I walked up the hill towards the Institute, for I wished very much to see Waddie, and learn what his father had said about my taking the agency of the Lake Shore Line.

CHAPTER XVI.

THE UCAYGA IN TROUBLE.

IT was nearly noon when I reached the Institute grounds, and, as the forenoon session would soon be over, I waited for Waddie to come out. I could not help smiling, as I recalled the stiff look of the colonel when I met him. But I was pleased to see that he appeared better than usual. His face was not so red, and it was easy to believe that he had tippled in moderation, if at all, since our visit to Grass Springs. Waddie joined me when the bell rang, and put an end to my moral reflections. We walked together into the grove to get away from the rest of the students.

"What did your father say, Waddie?" I asked, opening the subject which was uppermost in my thought.

"He is rather non-committal," replied my friend. "He says it is for you to do as you think proper."

"Did he make no objection?"

"He said, if you could accept any position on the Lake Shore Line after what had passed between you, he should have nothing to say."

By "what had passed between us" I judged that he meant the check for ten thousand dollars; but, if he had made the inquiry at the bank, he must have known that the check had not been presented for payment.

"Was that all?"

"Every word. He didn't want to say anything; and I dragged this out of him."

"That is not very satisfactory," I replied.

"You are a queer fellow, Wolf!" laughed Waddie, stepping back a couple of paces. "After my father has discharged you, without any explanation, and told you to regard him as a stranger, you want to ask his permission to accept another situation."

"I don't ask his permission. I only want to know what he thinks of it. I don't wish to stir up the old rivalry again. If I can quietly take the place offered me, I should like to do so."

"Take it, Wolf, and ask no more questions," said he, as we walked towards the town.

I was far from satisfied. I could not mention the check the colonel had given me, and which I had destroyed; but this was the key to the whole matter between the magnate and myself. It was necessary for him to know that I had destroyed the check, and the reasons why I had done so. If I wrote to him to this effect, I had no doubt that he would send me another check for the same sum; for nothing could be more offensive to him than for me to say he had drawn the check when he was not in condition to do business. If it had been for a hundred thousand dollars, he would have insisted on paying the money, rather than admit the mortifying truth. If he insisted on compensating me with this large sum for my discharge, why should I refuse to take it? I was poor and proud. The money looked like "hush-money," and I was afraid it would burn my fingers.

I decided to write to the colonel a true statement in regard to the check, without alluding to any other subject. If he sent me another, I would return it, with the assurance that whatever had been confidential between us would remain so, but my silence could not be purchased. I was not the magnate of

Centreport, or of Middleport; but, so far as anything which looked dishonorable or belittling was concerned, I was as proud as either of them. Having reached a conclusion which was quite satisfactory to me, I parted with Waddie, and walked towards the bank.

It is said that the evil one is always near when you speak of him; but it is more true that the angels are near when you think of them. As I walked along I met Captain Portman, of whom I had thought several times while at work in the garden, and whom I intended to visit if my involuntary vacation was prolonged. He invited me to dine with him at the hotel, and we were on our way thither, when Waddie Wimpleton, driving one of his father's horses, drew up in the street beside us.

"I want you, Wolf," said he, in excited tones.

"What's the matter?" I inquired.

"Jump in, and I will tell you," he replied, impatiently.

"I have just accepted an invitation to dine with Captain Portman," I added.

"Perhaps he will be kind enough to excuse you to-day."

"Certainly, if you desire," said my friend, in a low tone.

"I will return, if possible," I answered, as I jumped into the buggy with Waddie.

I was satisfied that something important had happened, and I was curious to know what it was.

"The Ucayga is aground in the Horse Shoe Channel!" said Waddie, as he started.

"Indeed! I am very sorry to hear it," I replied; and my first thought was of Van Wolter, who had all my sympathy in his misfortune.

"It's so. She went on this morning, at a little after nine, and they have been at work ever since, trying to get her off."

"I am sorry for the captain."

"He will kill the line in a month," replied Waddie, fretfully. "He missed his connection yesterday, and now the boat is aground."

"Van Wolter is a first-rate man."

"He's a first-rate man, but he isn't fit for captain."

"I don't know about that. The Horse Shoe Channel is all that troubles him."

"Well, he must go through there in order to be on

time. He lost the trains yesterday by going round the South Shoe."

"But where are you going?" I inquired, for Waddie had turned his horse, and was driving furiously towards the steamboat wharf.

"I want you to go up and get her off."

"Me!" I exclaimed. "I don't know that I can get her off."

"I know you can," added Waddie, confidently. "She will stay there till doomsday if you don't get her off."

"O, come, Waddie, you are rather extravagant in your ideas," I protested. "If Captain Van Wolter cannot get her off, I shall not be likely to succeed any better."

"You can get her off, if you will. Everybody says you can. The passengers are still on board, as mad as maniacs at the detention. They say they will never go in the Ucayga again till you are restored."

"You are making it rather strong, Waddie."

"I'm not! By the great horn spoon, I'm only telling you just what the messenger that came down for assistance says. They are firing up the old tow-boat, and you must go down with me in her."

"I am willing to go, so far as I am concerned, though it is rather embarrassing to have so much expected of a fellow as you require of me. What does your father say?"

"I haven't seen him. He has gone down to Gulfport, I believe. I was unanimously elected president of the Steamboat Company, and I am going to get her out of the scrape without waiting the return of my father," continued Waddie, earnestly.

"I am not willing to go down without his knowledge and consent, especially if there is any dissatisfaction among the passengers. Your father might say I went down to make trouble. If he wishes me to go, I will."

"But he is not here."

"He will be back, perhaps, before the tow-boat is ready to start. She can't get off under an hour."

"Very well; I will see him."

"In the mean time, I will go over to Middleport. I will return by half past two."

Reluctantly he consented to my plan; and I borrowed the Raven of him, in which to cross the lake. I was willing to believe, with Waddie, that the steamboat line would be ruined in a short time if these accidents were repeated. I was sorry for poor Van Wolter, and I could not imagine how he had contrived to get aground. It did not seem to me I could have done so if I had tried. I was going over to Middleport for a purpose. The tow-boat on which they were getting up steam was a wheezy old thing, and I was confident she could do nothing to help the Ucayga out of her trouble, even if they had anybody on board who knew the channel well enough to get her through the passage to the place where the Ucayga lay.

The Horse Shoe Channel had never been used by steamers till I took the Ucayga through it. There was not a pilot on the lake who was familiar with its bearings except Van Wolter and myself. As the unfortunate boat had taken the ground in going down the lake, and at the point where the channel bends between the Horse Shoe and the North Shoe, it was necessary to approach her in the same way, for she could only be hauled off the shoal in the opposite direction from that she had gone upon it.

I crossed the lake, and hastened to the house of Major Toppleton. I saw Tommy first, and told him the news. A year before he would have rejoiced at it; now he was apparently sorry. I told him that the accident afforded a splendid opportunity for his father to do a magnanimous deed. He listened to me with deep interest, while I proposed that the Ruoara, the railroad boat which arrived from Hitaca at half past two, should go down to the assistance of the Ucayga. It would be returning "good for evil;" it would be an illustration of the divine precept, "Love your enemies." Tommy was delighted with the suggestion, but he was doubtful whether his father would consent to it. We went together to see him. He laughed at us at first; but we argued the case very earnestly, and were assisted by Mrs. Toppleton and Grace. We carried the point at last, and he wrote an order placing the boat at my disposal for three hours, for she must return in season to take the passengers up the lake. It was nearly two when I embarked in the Raven to cross back to Centreport. Waddie was on the wharf, very nervous, when I arrived.

"I have seen my father," said he, as soon as I came within hailing distance of him.

"What does he say?" I asked, as I came up to the wharf.

"He would not say anything about you, but he told me I might get the boat off the best way I could; and I am going to have you do it."

"I am satisfied with this arrangement," I answered, and proceeded to explain the provision I had made on the other side to meet the emergency.

The tow-boat was all ready, and Waddie was impatient to be off. I told him to send her along, and we should overtake her before she reached the channel. We crossed at once to Middleport in the Raven, for the Ruoara was coming, a little ahead of her time. The order was delivered to the captain, and in a short time the boat was headed down the lake. From the statement of Waddie I knew just where the Ucayga lay. Van Wolter had hugged the shore a little too closely in going round the bend of the channel, and had run his bow into the sand. I used all my time in studying the situation, and the means to be used for getting the boat off, and I was

THE UCAYGA IN TROUBLE. Page 183.

reasonably confident that I should be able to realize Waddie's high hope of my ability.

When we passed the tow-boat, I told Waddie to send her round the Horse Shoe, and let her come up the channel from the north, because her captain could not take her through the narrow passage. I took the wheel of the Ruoara, and backed her through the channel myself, stopping her wheels just astern of the grounded steamer. I then took a jolly-boat, with a couple of deck hands to row, and hastened to examine the position of the steamer. Waddie went with me, because he was too nervous, to remain idle while anything was going on.

The position of the Ucayga had been correctly described to me. She had run her bow upon the sands which bordered the sides of the channel, and was listed over on the port side. As my boat pulled towards her bow, the crowd of passengers on board of her rushed forward to see what was to be done.

"Three cheers for Captain Wolf Penniman!" shouted some one on the deck; and the cheers were given with a will that confounded me; for, as I have said twenty times before, I am a modest man, and applause embarrasses me.

I continued my survey of the position of the Ucayga, as though I did not understand the cheers; but they were repeated, and I was obliged to take off my cap and acknowledge the salute, which seemed to satisfy my friends. I then went on board the steamer, to consult with Captain Van Wolter.

CHAPTER XVII.

AN ACT OF COURTESY.

"CAPTAIN PENNIMAN, I have been tempted to jump overboard and drown myself," said Van Wolter, as he grasped my hand when I stepped on board of the Ucayga.

His face was the impersonation of abject misery, and I realized that he was suffering intensely.

"Don't take it so hard, captain," I replied, pressing his hand. "Accidents do happen to the best of men."

"I am ruined!" groaned he.

"Not at all! There is no ruin about it. How did it happen?"

"I hardly know. I suppose I gave her a little too much helm, and she got to swinging."

"Did you stop her wheels?"

"Yes; but I had to hug the port side to keep her from swinging, and then she ran on."

"She has gone on pretty hard, I see."

"Yes, she has; I have done everything I could to haul her off; but she sticks tight."

"You had nothing to work with, and you could hardly expect to get her off. But what have you done?" I inquired.

"I have doubled up all the hawsers, and carried them ashore to that tree on the Shooter. Then we heaved on the capstan, till the hawser parted. But I have tied the parts together, and we were going to try again just as you came."

"All right. That's a good idea," I added.

"But I don't see what you can do with that boat in the Horse Shoe Channel. If you attempt to haul us off with her, you must keep her in the deep water, and that will only pull us on the harder."

"I think we can manage that," I replied, moving towards the engine-room, where my father was in charge.

The passengers crowded around me, and not a few of them were unkind enough to say things which must have wounded the feelings of Van Wolter. I found that my father had kept steam up, and I told him in brief the plan upon which I intended to operate. I have said before that I had always been a diligent student in scientific subjects, especially in the department of mechanics and machinery. I am confident now that I could never have taken the Ucayga through the narrow and curving channel of the Horse Shoe without the information thus obtained; and it was the want of this scientific knowledge which had caused Van Wolter to run the boat on the shore. He knew the channel, and had the bearings, but he had made his blunder in handling the boat.

"Now, captain, we will go to work," said I. "Let your men bring that hawser to the shaft."

He promptly followed my directions, without asking any questions.

"Pass the rope under and over the shaft. Give it about three turns," I continued.

"I see the idea," replied Van Wolter; "but I am afraid the hawser will part."

"You must not let it part. If it strains too hard, ease it off," I answered, giving him a fuller explanation of my plan.

Having seen the hawser properly adjusted, I returned to the jolly-boat at the bow. While I was engaged at the shaft, Waddie had been talking with the passengers, and as he joined me, I heard him assure a group of them that I should be restored to my former position.

"You must not be too fast, Waddie," said I, as the boat pulled towards the tug, which had by this time arrived at the upper end of the channel.

"I am not too fast."

"I think you are. You are very kind; but I am not sure that your promises can be redeemed."

"If they cannot be, the Steamboat Line is ruined. The passengers say they will never go in the Ucayga again while she is under her present management; and I don't blame them either," added Waddie, warmly.

"But I am not sure that your father will consent to any change."

"He must consent."

We boarded the tug-boat, which was plentifully supplied with hawsers for towing canal-boats. I ran her under the starboard quarter of the Ucayga, and carried off a stout rope, which was made fast to a big cleat on deck. I pointed out a barn on the main shore, and directed the captain to run for it when I gave him the signal.

Taking one of the tow-boat's heaviest hawsers into the boat, the end of which had been made fast at the stern of the Ucayga, I carried it to the Ruoara, where it was secured. By the several arrangements I had made, four different forces were to act upon the grounded steamer — her own paddles, the hawser on her shaft, made fast to the tree on the Shooter, the line to the tow-boat, and the one to the Ruoara. The last two, however, were to form a compound force. The tug-boat was to pull at right angles with the keel of the Ucayga, while the Ruoara was to act, at an acute angle, on the opposite side of the keel. The latter line would haul her more on the sand, while the former would pull her square off. The resultant of these two forces would carry her in the direction opposite that in which she had run on the bank. The hawser fastened to the tree, and the Ucayga's wheels, would both act in the same direction.

Returning to the jolly-boat again, I took position near the grounded steamer, where the captains of the three boats could see me. I had told the mate of the Ruoara to steer for a point which would keep him in the channel. At the word from me, all three steamers were to start their wheels, the Ucayga back, and the other two forward.

"Are you all ready?" I shouted.

"All ready," replied the captains, one after another.

"Go ahead!" I called.

I confess that my heart beat wildly as the wheels of the three steamers began to turn. I had laid my plan very carefully, and a minute more was to decide whether it was success or failure. The hawser to the tree straightened, strained, and groaned, and the water splashed and rolled behind the wheels of the boat.

"She moves!" cried Captain Van Wolter; and I thought I could hear the keel grate upon the sand.

The moment the Ucayga felt the full force of the power exerted, she slid off the bank and righted. The crowd of passengers on deck gave three deafening cheers.

"Stop her!" I shouted, at the top of my lungs, at the same time making violent gestures to the three boats.

The order was promptly obeyed.

"Go ahead, Ucayga!" I continued, fearful that she would take the ground on the other side of the channel.

Van Wolter started the wheels, and checked her; but she lay obliquely across the channel, where it was impossible to start her.

"Cast off the hawser on the quarter!" I called to Van Wolter, as my boat pulled under the Ucayga's counter. "Go ahead, Ruoara!" I added, to the captain of this boat.

The Ruoara went ahead until I told her to stop, and the effect was to haul the stern of the Ucayga round, so that she lay square in the channel. After the hawser to the tree had been cast off, I went on board of her, and hastening to my accustomed place in the wheel-house, I started her ahead, taking the helm myself. As she had no headway on, it was not necessary to hug the port side of the channel as closely as usual — an apparent neglect which bothered Van Wolter. I explained to him the reasons for my action, assuring him that the only difficulty in going through the passage was in correctly providing for the swing of the boat.

"I shall never take her through there again," said he.

"You will soon get the hang of it," I replied, as I rang to stop her. "I will help you."

"Are you not going down with us?"

"No; I must return to Centreport. You can go round the Horse Shoe on your up trip," I answered, as I hastened to the jolly-boat, which was towing astern.

The passengers greeted me very warmly, and said ever so many complimentary things; but I did not want to hear any of them. I assured them that they were in season for the afternoon trains; and Waddie and I leaped into the boat, which pulled for the Ruoara. As we passed the tug-boat, she was directed to return to Centreport. I piloted the steamer in which I had come up out of the narrow passage, and we arrived at Middleport in ample season for her to make her trip up the lake.

Major Toppleton and Tommy were on the wharf when we landed, and I informed them of the success of the plan we had adopted. The father seemed to be a little nervous; and I think he was really pleased with what he had done, though his pride would not permit him to say so.

"Do you think your father would do as much for me, Waddie, if one of my boats got aground?" said he, after we had discussed the matter.

"I am afraid not, sir; but I would," replied Waddie.

"Give my regards to your father, and tell him I am glad the Ucayga has got off," added the major, laughing, so that we could not tell whether he was in jest or in earnest.

"I will, with pleasure, sir," answered Waddie, as the major left the spot.

"Does he mean it?" asked Waddie, after musing a moment.

"I don't know," I replied.

"Neither do I," said Tommy; "but I have sometimes thought that, if Colonel Wimpleton would meet him half way, he would be glad to heal up all the old sores."

"Well, I must go home," continued Waddie. "Good by."

"Hold on; I am going over with you," I interposed. "I have your father's check, which I intended to draw, though I suppose the bank is closed by this time."

"No matter if it is. You shall have your money, if they have to open the bank for you."

I went over with him in the Raven, more because I wanted to hear what people said on the other side than because I was anxious to get my money that day. Colonel Wimpleton was on the wharf, talking with the captain of the tug-boat, which had just arrived. He had heard the result of the efforts to relieve the Ucayga by this time, and the captain appeared to be giving him the details of the movement. He saw me as we landed, but he took no notice of me.

"Major Toppleton sends his regards to you, and says he is glad the Ucayga has been got off," said Waddie.

"What!" exclaimed the magnate, his cheeks reddening.

His son repeated the message, and I waited with intense interest to observe the effect upon him. To my surprise, he did not go into a passion, though I saw him frown, — perhaps from the force of habit. For my own part, I could not see how the colonel, after this kind and conciliatory act by his rival, could say or think any harsh thing. It was true we, the young peacemakers, had rather extorted the courteous deed from the major; but it had been done.

"Did you pay for the use of the boat?" asked the colonel, after frowning and pursing up his lips for a moment, as if to hide his vexation.

"No, sir; certainly not. It would have been little less than an insult to offer to pay for what was done simply as an act of courtesy."

Colonel Wimpleton was evidently very much troubled; but, instead of pursuing the matter any farther, he began to question the captain of the tow-boat in regard to the event of the day. I did not consider myself justified in listening to the conversation, and so I walked up the wharf. Waddie followed me.

CHAPTER XVIII.

THE MYSTERY OF THE CHECK.

"I WILL go with you to the bank, and see that you get your money, Wolf," said Waddie.

"What does your father think about the boat?"

"I don't know. It is impossible to tell what he thinks about anything of this kind. If he had known of it in season, he would not have permitted us to ask the major for the use of the Ruoara. He would have let the Ucayga rot in the sand before he would have done it."

"Major Toppleton stands first rate, just now," I added.

"He would make up, I think, if my father would."

We discussed the matter on our way to the bank, and both of us were hopeful that some good would come out of the event of the day. The bank was closed; but the cashier was in the room, at work upon his books and papers. I handed him my check. Waddie requested him to pay it, and then walked into another room.

"I paid a pretty large check in your favor to-day, Captain Penniman," said he, with a smile, as he took the one I gave him.

"In my favor!" I exclaimed, confounded by the statement, and rather inclined to think he was quizzing me.

"Yes; ten thousand dollars."

"You don't mean so!"

"Certainly I do," answered the cashier, very good-naturedly, I thought, considering that there was a suspicion of something wrong about the matter.

"I think you are joking, sir."

"Not at all. I am entirely serious," he added, still smiling.

I was not intimate enough with the bank officer to be on joking terms with him; but the persistent smile he wore, after I had intimated that I knew nothing about the check, seemed to indicate that he did not mean what he said. I had destroyed the check which Colonel Wimpleton gave me, and of course it was not possible that the cashier had paid it. I was quite sure that I had burned the valuable paper, and even scattered the tinder after it had been destroyed.

"Am I to understand, sir, that you paid a check for ten thousand dollars in my favor?" I demanded, rather warmly.

"That is precisely what I did," answered the cashier, squarely.

"And to me?"

"Certainly not to you in person."

"Who presented it?"

"Van Wolter."

"What, the mate of the Ucayga — or rather the captain?" I continued, beginning to be somewhat excited.

"No; to his son — Nick Van Wolter," replied the cashier, who obstinately persisted in being calm, and 'n wearing a smiling face, notwithstanding my conduct must have convinced him that something was wrong.

"I can only say that somebody has been swindling you."

"O, no, I think not. Of course I should not pay such a large sum to a young man like Nick Van Wolter without making sure that there was no mistake. I took the check to Colonel Wimpleton, who told me it was all right, ordered me to pay it, and say nothing about it to any one," replied the official, whose name was Barnes, with a very significant smile.

"It's a fraud, sir!" I protested, vehemently.

"Please don't speak so loud. Waddie is in the directors' room, and may hear you. I understood, from what Colonel Wimpleton said, that this affair was to be private between you and him."

"Private! But I tell you I sent no check, and I have not seen the money," I replied.

"You need not be afraid of me, Captain Penniman. The secret is safe with me. Nick said you sent him because you did not wish any one to know that the colonel paid you so much money."

"I don't understand you, sir. I have never spoken a word to Nick about a check, much less sent him to cash one for me. I tell you there is something wrong about this business."

"What's the matter?" demanded Waddie, returning to the banking-room. "Can't you pay the check, Mr. Barnes?"

"Certainly, Waddie; there is no trouble about that. We were speaking of another matter," answered the cashier. "Here is the evening paper."

Waddie took the paper, and returned to the directors' room.

"I do not see how there can be anything wrong about the business, when Colonel Wimpleton declared that the check was good, and ordered me to pay it."

"But I say, sir, so far as I am concerned, the business is all wrong. I had nothing whatever to do with it, and don't know anything about it."

"Let me ask you one question: Did or did not Colonel Wimpleton give you a check for ten thousand dollars?" continued Mr. Barnes, who had begun to be a little perplexed himself.

"He did, but —"

"Very well; and I paid it."

"No, sir; you did not. I burned the check, and took pains to scatter even the ashes of it. I don't understand it, sir."

"I don't know that it makes any difference whether you understand it or not. You acknowledge that the colonel gave you a check for ten thousand dollars. I have paid one for that amount, in your favor, and the colonel examined the check, and declared that it was all right."

"That may satisfy you, but it does not satisfy me," I added.

"It is plain enough, Captain Penniman, that your relations with our friend the colonel are disturbed. He is as careful to conceal the existence of this check as you are. It seems to me nothing more need be said about it. The secret is safe in my keeping, for I do not even enter your name on the books of the bank. The check is cancelled, and will be returned to Colonel Wimpleton on the first of the month, when I balance his account."

"Mr. Barnes, do you regard me as a liar?" I demanded, indignantly.

"Certainly not."

"Then I say again, that I have sent no check to the bank, and I have not received the money you paid."

"That is your lookout."

"Will you let me see the check?"

"Of course."

He took the paper from a drawer, and handed it to me. There was no doubt in my mind that it was a genuine check. The truth suddenly flashed upon me. This was the first check which Colonel Wimpleton had drawn at the hotel; the one which had disappeared, and for which I had made such diligent search in and around the house. I came to the conclusion at the time that the magnate had torn it up with the pledge I had written, though I had been unable to find any of the pieces.

"Do you understand it now?" asked the cashier.

"I am beginning to have an idea," I replied, returning to him the cancelled check. "Where may I see you again this evening, sir?"

"At my house," he replied, indicating the locality of it.

I was afraid to detain Waddie any longer, and unwilling to intrust him with his father's secret. We walked down to the wharf together, and there I parted with him. He assured me that on the next morning I should be called to the command of the Ucayga again.

I got into my skiff; but I could not go home with the mystery of the check unsolved; and I sat on the thwart, considering the circumstances connected with it. I recalled all the events of my visit to Grass Springs. I had left the check on the table with the paper I had written. The colonel tore up the latter, and threw the pieces out the window, while I was walking back and forth in the room. I then followed him to the bar-room, where he had procured a glass of brandy. He wished to go to the Horse Shoe, and insisted that I should accompany him. Happening to think of the check, I returned to the room for it, but could not find it. I told the colonel that it had disappeared, and I went out doors to see if I could identify any of the pieces. While I was looking for them I met Nick Van Wolter. When I returned to the colonel, he had drawn up the second check.

Nick was at the hotel while I was in the room with the drunken magnate. He told me he had spoken with the landlord about my patient. Therefore he had been in the house. It was possible, and subsequent events rendered it probable, that he had gone into the colonel's chamber while we were at the bar. Seeing the check upon the table, he had taken it. This was the only theory I could devise to explain the mystery. But all this could, perhaps, be demonstrated, and I decided to see Nick at once. I hastened to his father's house. On my way I could not help recalling Waddie's strong saying, that Nick was a snake.

I knocked at the door, and Mrs. Van Wolter answered the summons; but she informed me that her son had gone up to Hitaca by the afternoon boat. He expected to obtain a situation there as clerk in one of the hotels, and had taken all his clothes with him. If I wanted him, she would send for him. I left the house. If Nick had obtained ten thousand dollars, he would not be likely to stay long in Centreport. I walked excitedly to the house of the cashier; but he had not yet returned from the bank, and I sought him there.

"Well, captain, have you obtained any light?" he inquired, as I entered.

"Yes, sir; I have. Nick Van Wolter is a thief and a swindler!" I replied, warmly.

"The loss comes on you, and not on the bank," added the prudent man of money.

"It can hardly come on me, since I never had the money to lose, though that makes but little difference. Something must be done."

"Have you seen Colonel Wimpleton?"

"No, sir; I have not. As you suggested, our relations are disturbed," I replied.

"He is at home this evening, and you certainly ought to inform him of the facts in this case. But I cannot see how, if he gave you a check for ten thousand dollars, and you destroyed it, that same check could have been presented at the bank to-day for payment," said Mr. Barnes, with a significant smile. "It seems to me utterly impossible."

"It was not the same check. Colonel Wimpleton will understand that part of the story, if you do not. I do not feel at liberty to explain it; he may, if he pleases. I will write a note to him, if you will give me pen and paper."

The cashier gave me a seat at his desk, and I wrote a full statement of what I had done with the check he had given me, adding that Nick Van Wolter had stolen the one paid that day. I told him I had no desire to disobey his commands, and would not have done so under any other circumstances. I concluded by saying that, if the money was to be used at all, it belonged to me. I should consider that Nick had stolen it from me, and I should have him arrested. I proposed to pursue him, in the absence of any directions from the colonel. I should be at the bank for half an hour, and would receive his answer there, if he wished to make any reply. The cashier sent the letter by the porter to the house of the magnate.

"They say you are going to have the command of the steamer again, Captain Penniman," said Mr. Barnes, after the messenger had gone.

"I don't know about that; I don't think so myself."

"Van Wolter don't make out very well."

"He will do very well indeed, except in the Horse Shoe Channel. I think he is a first-rate man, obliging and reliable. I am sorry his son is not more like him."

"He is more like his mother than his father. There has been a great deal of talk about Colonel Wimpleton lately," added the cashier, evidently intending to lead the conversation into that channel.

Fortunately for me, — for I was not willing to be questioned in regard to my relations with the great man, — the messenger returned very soon, and delivered a note to me. Eagerly I opened it, and found only a single line: "I will see you in my library immediately." This was entirely satisfactory, and I hastened to his house.

CHAPTER XIX.

COLONEL WIMPLETON HUMILIATED.

COLONEL WIMPLETON was alone in his library when I reached the house. He made a gesture towards a chair, but he was as stiff in his manner as he had been when I met him that day in the street. Yet, in spite of this display of dignity, I could see that he was troubled. He looked rather pale, and the toddy-blossoms on his nose were in stronger contrast than usual with the rest of his face. If I read him right, he was sorely vexed and perplexed.

"I received your note, Wolf," said he, struggling, I thought, to appear colder and stiffer than he really felt. "I am astonished at its contents."

"I supposed you would be, sir," I replied.

"Am I to believe that you destroyed the check I gave you?" demanded he, sternly.

"That is the simple truth."

"Wolf, I have always believed you were honest, whatever else you may have been; but this story is incredible."

"I grant that it looks very strange, but it is none the less true because it is strange. You remember that you wrote two checks on the day we were at the hotel in Grass Springs."

"Of course I remember it," answered he, petulantly, as though he deemed the question an intimation that he was not in condition at the time to remember it. "I tore up the first one, by accident, with the paper you wrote."

"Well, sir, I was not sure at the time that you did tear up the first one. I am satisfied now that you did not. I could not find a single piece of it."

"Humph! That may be."

"Nick Van Wolter was at the hotel that day. I met him in the street, when I was looking for the pieces of the check."

"When you sent him over— No matter about that, said he, suddenly checking himself.

But he had said enough to assure me that Nick

had told him something; and I was now willing to believe that the fellow was really the snake Waddie had declared he was.

"I met him in the street," I continued, without heeding the slip the magnate had made. "He told me he had been into the hotel, and had seen the landlord. I am confident he went into the room where we were, and took the check."

"It don't look probable."

"You wrote the check in a book you carried in your pocket," I proceeded, hoping I should be able to convince him of the truth of what I said.

"I did," he replied, taking the check-book from his pocket.

"When you had written it, you tore it out?"

"Yes, in this place;" and he pointed out the leaf in his check-book, on which he had made the marginal memorandum. "I tore the first check from this margin, and here is the amount, and 'Steamer,' indicating for what purpose it was paid."

"Where is the place from which you tore the second check?" I asked, anxiously.

"As the second was a duplicate, I wrote it at the

end of the book, and made no memorandum in the margin," he replied, turning to one of the last leaves in the volume.

"Now, sir, I think you have the means of convincing yourself that it was the first check, and not the second, which was paid at the bank to-day," I continued. "That margin, where you tore off the first check, is rather rough and uneven. The edge of the check will correspond to it."

"We will go to the bank, if Mr. Barnes is there," said the colonel, more interested than I supposed he would be.

We walked to the bank, and the cashier handed him the check. The edge where it had been torn off was very irregular, and the colonel adjusted it against the margin. It exactly fitted, as I knew it would, and he could not escape the conclusion that the first, and not the second check had been used. I felt then that I had vindicated my veracity, and I was satisfied. The magnate told the cashier that he had drawn duplicate checks, and believed the first had been destroyed; that my story was true, in short; but he wished nothing said. He then told me to return to his house with him.

"Wolf, I would rather give ten thousand dollars than have this matter stirred up," said the colonel, when we were again seated in the library. "It has already given me a great deal of trouble and uneasiness."

"But you do not intend to let Nick Van Wolter run away with ten thousand dollars — do you?" I inquired.

"Has he run away?"

"Yes, sir; I have no doubt he has. His mother says he has gone to Hitaca to take a situation in a hotel, and carried his clothes with him; but I warrant he will not stay long in Hitaca."

"He is a scoundrel, then."

"Undoubtedly he is."

Colonel Wimpleton walked up and down the room in deep thought. I did not know then what troubled him; but I learned the truth before morning.

"What can be done?" he asked, pausing before me.

"Pursue and arrest him."

The great man pursed up his lips, and did not seem to like the advice.

"That would stir up the whole affair," said he.

"What affair, sir?" I asked.

"He stole the check at Grass Springs. I should not like to listen to the testimony which would be brought forward to prove that Nick was there that day," answered the colonel, with a sickly smile.

"We need not arrest him, then. You can compel him to give up the money," I suggested.

"Can we catch him?"

"I don't think he got away from Hitaca last night. The train south leaves at twenty minutes past seven. When I ran the Ucayga, I hurried her up so that we were in season for it; but she was late yesterday afternoon, and I know she lost it."

"But he may have left by some other conveyance."

"There is no other, unless he took a private vehicle. If he did that, we can easily trace him. But I think he will take the eleven o'clock train, south, to-morrow forenoon. He will not expect any discovery at once, and will not hurry himself. He knows very well that there is no conveyance to Hitaca till to-morrow forenoon, and he will be a hundred miles off before the next boat arrives there."

"How shall we get there? I don't like to drive twenty-five miles in the night. I am not very well," replied the colonel.

"We will go in the Belle if you please. You can take one of the berths, and go to bed. There is a good breeze, and we shall be in Hitaca in three or four hours."

"Very well; I will do so. Who goes with you?"

"Tom Walton."

"Is it necessary that he should go with you?"

"No, sir."

"I wish to talk with you about other matters," he added, with an air of embarrassment, "and do not wish for any listeners."

"I will be alone then, sir."

Fluttering with excitement, I left him, promising to be at the wharf with the Belle in an hour. I crossed the lake, found Tom Walton, and told him I wanted the boat till the next night. Fortunately she was not engaged, though a gentleman had spoken about a cruise up the lake in her. Tom went down, and put her in order for the trip, while I went home to tell my father and mother where I was going. My father was very curious to know what was going on; but I could only stop long enough to tell him that I thought everything was coming around right again. As the check was the key to all the other secrets between the colonel and myself, I did not dare allude to it.

Sailing the Belle across the lake, I found Colonel Wimpleton on the wharf, muffled in his overcoat. Tom had lighted the cabin, and it was all ready for the reception of my passenger; but he preferred a seat with me in the standing-room. Shoving off, I headed the boat up the lake, and she soon began to fly over the waves, under the influence of the fresh north wind. Colonel Wimpleton was silent for a time. Since I first met him, early in the evening, I had been impressed by his altered manner. Something apparently weighed heavy upon his mind, and he appeared to be struggling, with the pride of his character, to conceal it.

"Wolf, this is bad business," said he, when the Belle was approaching Gulfport.

"Bad for Nick Van Wolter, sir," I replied.

"For me too," he added, after a long pause. "I

would not have this matter stirred up for double the sum Nick has stolen. It is better for me to give you another check, and let the scoundrel go."

"I have no claim upon you, sir, for such a sum. You are very generous, and I ought to be the last one to impose upon your kindness."

"Why didn't you draw the check, and not burn it?"

"I did not think it was right for me to take so much money under the circumstances. Pardon me, sir; I do not like to allude to the matter again."

"If you had drawn the check the next day, there would have been no trouble. If Nick had his check then, I don't see why he did not collect it."

"I haven't been over to Centreport since the day I was dismissed, and perhaps he thought it would not be safe to present it, unless he knew I was in town. I met him when I first came over, and he drew the check as soon as he had seen me."

"It is a pity you burned the check," mused the magnate.

I did not care to remind him of the unpleasant affair at Grass Springs, and I kept still.

"Wolf, tell me candidly why you burned that check," said he, after a silence of several minutes.

"I did not think it was right for me to use it. If my father or mother found it upon me, I could not tell how I came by it. I might lose it, and some one else get the money," I answered.

"But why did you think it was not right for you to use it?" he inquired.

"I do not like to explain."

"Do so; I will not be angry."

"Well, sir, I did not think you were in condition to do business; and if it were known that I drew the check, people would think I had been swindling you. It was partly for your sake and partly for my own that I destroyed it."

"In my note to you the next day, I wrote that the check would be paid."

"I had already destroyed it then."

There was another long pause in the conversation, though two or three times the colonel began to speak, and then checked himself. It was plain to me that he was struggling to utter something at which his pride revolted, and though I was very curious to know what was coming, I deemed it prudent to keep still.

"Wolf, I have been terribly humiliated," said he, with a desperate effort. "I have suffered intolerably since that affair at the Springs. That one of my employés, a mere boy, should tell me I was drunk,— *drunk;* that's the word,—has made me miserable."

"I am sorry—"

"Don't apologize, Wolf," he interposed. "It is not so much that you said it, as because it was true."

He uttered the words with a long and heavy sigh; and really he was so sad that I could not help pitying him.

"I am sorry it was true; but—"

"Hear me, Wolf. You have said to me what no other living being ever said to me, or would have dared to say."

"I hope you will excuse me, sir. It was very bold in me to say it, even if it was true."

"Wolf, I haven't drank a drop since that night. I never will drink another drop," he continued, taking no notice of my apologies and explanations. "To put it in the power of any one to look down upon me is too humiliating. I have done it once, I never will do it again."

How far his conscience reproached him I had no means of knowing, for he attributed his suffering wholly to mortified pride. He was silent again, and I thought it would be impudence in me to commend his good resolution; but certainly nothing ever afforded me more pleasure, for I knew that his natural firmness, amounting to obstinacy, would keep him true to his pledge.

CHAPTER XX.

A NIGHT TRIP TO HITACA.

IT seemed to me that pride had had a terrible fall in the person of Colonel Wimpleton, though in the better sense it was pride's conquest over the low and degrading.

"I will not sign any paper, Wolf; but I mean what I say," said he, apparently feeling better for the confession he had made.

"I know you do, sir."

"I am aware, now, that three times on that day I was saved from injury or death by others. First my horse ran away with me."

"Your horse?"

"You shall know all, Wolf. I had drank so much in Ruoara, that I dropped the reins in driving home. In trying to recover them, I frightened the horse, and he ran with me. Nick stopped him. Then I came very near being run over by the train, and drowned in the lake. It was all because I had been drinking too much. It was time for me to brake up."

That was the very expression my father had used in regard to him. It is not every drunkard who has the power to "brake up" when he realizes the peril of his condition. The colonel's revelation had given me a new light. He had seen Nick that forenoon. I asked him about it, and he acknowledged that the snake had informed him in regard to the "courting" at the Horse Shoe. I could not then understand Nick's motive for doing so, but I have since learned it.

"Do you know why I discharged you, Wolf?" asked the colonel.

"I supposed it was because you did not want one in your employ who had seen you — as you were that day."

"Partly for that, but more because you were working against me."

"Against you, sir?"

"Nick told me you sent him to the Horse Shoe to warn the party of my approach."

"I did not wish to have Waddie and Miss Minnie see you as you were then."

"You were right, Wolf; and I thank you for saving them that pain and shame," he added, warmly. "I had no idea of saying as much to you as I have; and I should not if Nick's rascality had not come to light. I gave that villain five hundred dollars."

"What for?" I inquired, astonished at the acknowledgment.

"For stopping my horse, for saving my life in the boat, and for — for keeping my secret."

"What secret?"

"That my horse ran away with me."

"He ought to have been satisfied with that, without trying to steal any more," I added, more disgusted than ever with the conduct of Nick.

The snake must have put in at Green Cove on his return from the Horse Shoe, and had stopped the colonel's horse in the road near it. Here he had told the great man the mischief that was in store for his daughter. I could not fathom the motive of Nick in this mean act. But really I did not trouble myself much about him. I was more interested in the colonel himself. I was amazed at the freedom with which he talked to me. It had evidently caused him a severe mental struggle to open the subject; but, after he had broken the way, it seemed to afford him great relief. He owned that he had suffered intensely since his late debauch, and I concluded that his confession even to me, with its accompanying resolution, eased his mind.

Probably the effects of his intemperance wore heavily upon him physically, and the sudden change in his habits tended to produce depression. I had heard my father say that what is called an appetite for intoxicating drinks has no relation whatever to the taste; but when a person accustomed to drink liquor, moderately or otherwise, discontinues its use, he suffers from a kind of aching void in his physical frame, which nothing but the fiery fluid can supply. The stimulus of life seems wanting, and the spirits are fearfully depressed. This was doubtless the condition of Colonel Wimpleton. Certainly it was something extraordinary which had produced this change of his very nature.

He told me my words, declaring that he was drunk, had been ringing in his ears ever since they were uttered. He was not aware at the time how intoxicated he was. It was when he came to think of it in his sober moments, and in the solitude of his chamber, that he realized his situation. He felt that he deserved the pity of his friends and the contempt of his enemies. He shuddered when he thought of the future, with the habit steadily increasing upon him. Even his social position and great wealth could not save him and his family from the shame and disgrace which cling to the sot. His pride, rather than his principle, saved him.

"Wolf, do you think people generally knew that I drank too much?" he inquired.

"I am sorry to say they did. It was common talk," I replied, candidly.

"I never suspected that any one knew it."

"On the very day that Nick stopped your horse, he said to me that you were on a regular bat."

"A what?"

"A regular bat; another would have said a spree."

"Is it possible I have sunk so low!" exclaimed he, with something like a groan. "I alone have been blind."

"I heard another say if you did not brake up, you would go to ruin."

"I did brake up on the day after we went to the Springs. I feel better to-night than I have since we parted after our return."

"Will you tell me, sir, why you gave me that check?" I ventured to ask.

"Because I felt that I was in your power. You told me I was drunk, and money makes friends."

"Did you intend to discharge me then?"

"No; though I did not like the idea of having one in my employ who could talk to me in that way. I did not decide to dismiss you till the next morning, after Nick had told me you were working against me. I took this as an excuse rather than a provocation. You may resume your position as captain of the steamer to-morrow."

"I am very grateful to you, sir; but I do not like to displace Van Wolter, after he has been appointed."

"But he is not fit for the place."

"As fit as any man on the lake. You cannot find a pilot who would take the Ucayga through the Horse Shoe Channel."

"Perhaps you are right; but we will talk of that another time," replied the colonel.

15

He was silent and thoughtful again. I permitted him to choose his own topic; but, as one good resolution begets another, I hoped soon to find him in a frame of mind which would allow me to introduce a matter which was still near my heart. The magnate did not speak again for half an hour. We were off Port Gunga, and I heard a clock on shore strike twelve. I suggested to the colonel that he could sleep very comfortably in the cabin of the Belle.

"I do not care to sleep, Wolf," he replied, still clinging to his meditations.

I did not venture to disturb him, and we were within five miles of Hitaca when he spoke again. I was fearful that he regretted having said so much, and was compensating for his freedom by his long-continued silence. My fear was groundless, for when he spoke again I realized that his thought had been progress.

"Wolf!" said he, and paused.

"Sir."

"I was never so astonished in my life as when I learned that Toppleton had sent his steamer to the relief of the Ucayga," he added.

"It was only an act of courtesy," I replied, my heart beating with emotion; for this was the topic upon which I wished to talk with him.

"Such acts of courtesy have not passed much between Toppleton and myself of late years. Then he even had the audacity to send me a message of congratulation on the safety of the boat."

"I have no doubt he was sincere."

Another long pause.

"Twenty years ago, Toppleton was a good fellow, and we were the best of friends," he continued.

"He has done a great deal for me; and, though he was sometimes unjust, I always felt very grateful to him."

"I suppose I have been very unjust to you sometimes, too."

"I never had any claims upon you or Major Toppleton, and perhaps I am not as competent to judge as a disinterested person would be."

"Toppleton has offered you a good place on the railroad."

"Yes, sir; a very good place," I answered, warmly.

"Would you rather be in his employ than mine?"

"No, sir."

"If you would, I ought not to object."

"I would rather be in the employ of both of you," I suggested.

"That cannot very well be."

"I think it can, sir."

"How?"

"Major Toppleton offers to appoint me agent for the Lake Shore Railroad. If you will also appoint me agent of the steamboat, I shall be in the employ of both."

"Agent for two rival lines!" exclaimed he. "That is absurd."

"Of course I mean that the two lines shall be united."

"You are at your old trick, Wolf," replied the colonel; but there was no bitterness in his tones.

"I honestly think it would be best for both lines, and best for the travelling public."

"But I don't want Toppleton to think I am ready to go down on my knees to him," said the colonel, with a little of his old spite.

"Why, sir, Major Toppleton has, by his act of

courtesy yesterday, opened the way for you to do a similar one. He has met you more than half way without a word from you."

"I suppose I can be as courteous as he can. If one of his boats gets into trouble, mine shall help her out; but I am not to be the first one to propose a union of the two lines."

"But he has already proposed it."

"I will think of it, Wolf; but I do think we are in a better condition to connect than ever before."

Not daring to push the matter too fast, I said no more. At about two in the morning the Belle reached the wharf at Hitaca. We went to the hotel where the colonel usually staid, and, calling up the landlord, took rooms and retired.

I was so weary that it was after eight when I waked. I went down, and I found the colonel had not yet appeared. I called him, and after breakfast we visited all the hotels, but obtained no tidings of Nick Van Wolter. I had intended to get up soon enough to go on board the Ucayga before she started, but I had overslept myself, and she had been gone an hour and a half when I got out of bed. I blamed myself for my neglect; but it could not be helped. However, there was no doubt that Nick had come up in the steamer, and was somewhere in Hitaca. We could only lie in wait for him at the railroad station.

The railway from Hitaca has to overcome a very steep grade, and to do this the train "beats" up the hills, first running ahead, then switching off and backing a considerable distance, and then going ahead again on its course, thus saving the grade in turning. It occurred to me that Nick might go out to one of these switches, and enter the cars when they stopped. Colonel Wimpleton was to take the train at the station in town, while I went out in a wagon to the switches. I left my team at the farther one, and walked back to the first on the track. My calculation was correct. Nick had evidently heard of us in Hitaca, and expected to dodge us in this way. I confronted him in the steep road near the first switch, as the train was seen in the distance.

Nick had a travelling bag in one hand, with a breech-loading rifle over his shoulder. He turned pale when I stepped into his path. I told him he

must go back to Hitaca with me. Then he showed fight; and, not liking the looks of his rifle, I sprang upon him, for I was in earnest. He struggled desperately to escape me, and we had a hard tussle; but I finally wrenched the weapon from him, and threw him on the ground. Seizing him by the collar, I held him down till the train had passed.

CHAPTER XXI.

WHAT HAPPENED IN THE ROAD.

AS soon as the train had passed, and Nick's chance to escape had eluded him, I released my grasp, and permitted him to rise.

"What do you mean by pitching into me in that way?" demanded Nick, puffing with the violence of his struggles.

"I have business with you," I replied, as much out of wind as he was.

I stood in the road, by the side of his travelling bag, resting upon the rifle. I had arranged with Colonel Wimpleton to get out at the second switch, and drive back the horse he would find near it, if I did not join him. He was to understand by this that I had captured the fugitive.

"What do you want of me?" asked Nick, when he had recovered his breath a little.

"You know very well what I want."

"No, I don't."

"You do."

"How should I know?"

"Your conscience, if nothing else, will tell you."

"It don't. I'm going to California."

"Not just yet, Nick. You will give up some of the money you have upon you before you go to California, or anywhere else."

"What money?" said he, snappishly; but I saw that his lip quivered.

"Ten thousand dollars that you stole from me," I replied, impatiently.

"I never knew you had so much money."

"You stole a check in my favor, for that sum, at the hotel in Grass Springs."

"I didn't take any check."

"It's no use to lie about it, Nick. The whole thing has come out. If you want to spend the next twenty years of your life in the state prison, deny it. Colonel Wimpleton will be here in a few moments," I added, as I heard the rattle of the wagon.

"Colonel Wimpleton!" exclaimed Nick.

"Here he comes," I continued, as the wagon began to descend the hill. "If you try to get away from me, I may find it necessary to break your head."

"You have him," said the colonel, as he stopped the horse, and got out of the wagon.

I picked up Nick's travelling bag, for I suspected that the money, or some part of it, was in it.

"Nick, we can make short work of this business," said the colonel, confronting my prisoner. "We haven't brought any officers with us, but we can obtain them when needed."

"What do you want of me, Colonel Wimpleton?" asked Nick. "You gave me five hundred dollars for what I did for you, and I'm going to California, to see if I can't do something."

"You may go to California, but you must give up the ten thousand dollars you stole first."

"I haven't any ten thousand dollars."

"Yes, you have; you stole my check for that amount. It's useless for you to deny it."

"I didn't expect this of you, Colonel Wimpleton," added Nick, trying to assume an air of injured innocence, in which, however, he was not successful, for he hardly understood the phases of that quality.

"Instead of sending an officer after you, Nick, I have come myself. You must acknowledge that this was considerate."

"I saved your life, Colonel Wimpleton."

"If you did, that is no reason why you should steal ten thousand dollars from me."

"Wolf says I took it from him."

"We will not quibble; it will come out of me in the end."

"If I have to go back to Centreport, I think there will be some talk about you, Colonel Wimpleton."

"If you go back, it will only be on your way to the penitentiary. Will you give up the money, or not?"

"What! the five hundred you gave me for pulling you out of the lake?" exclaimed Nick.

"No; the ten thousand you stole."

"I haven't it."

I grasped Nick by the collar, for I thought, from a movement he made, that he intended to run for the woods.

"We need not parley with him," I added. "We had better search him at once."

"Let me alone, Wolf!" cried Nick, beginning to struggle.

Colonel Wimpleton came to my assistance, though I did not need his help; for I was abundantly able to manage Nick, and we held him fast. He made an effort to release himself; but finding it fruitless, he began to be more reasonable.

"If you will produce the money, all right; if you won't, I shall search you," said the colonel.

"You have no right to do that," blubbered Nick, who was now able fully to comprehend the situation.

"I shall take the responsibility," added the colonel. "Let me tell you in the beginning, Nick, that I do not intend to prosecute you unless you compel me to do so. You must give up the money you obtained by fraud."

"I will, if you won't send me to jail," replied Nick.

"I will not send you to jail. I have not forgotten what you did for me a few days ago."

"I haven't the money with me. I will send it to you to-morrow, if you will let me go."

"I will not let you go. Were you going to California without your money? Where is it?"

"In my bag."

"Open your bag," said the colonel.

Finding that his only hope of escaping the penalty of his crime was by giving up the money, he obeyed. Opening his bag, he took from a roll of clothing a little package, carefully wrapped up in brown paper, and gave it to Colonel Wimpleton. The latter opened the parcel, and found that it really contained the bank notes, which he hastily counted.

"The money is all here, Wolf," said the colonel. "You may let him go now."

I released him; but he was not disposed to go.

"Are you really going to California, Nick?" I asked of him.

"I was going there; but I haven't money enough now to pay my fare out and back, if I don't find anything to do," he replied, doggedly; and it was plain that he was more disappointed than burdened with guilt at the failure of his plans.

"I will give you more, Nick," said the colonel; "for I think my life is worth more than five hundred dollars."

"I shouldn't have used this check if you had done the handsome thing by me," added Nick, with an effrontery which moved me to indignation.

"I will give you fifteen hundred dollars more," said the colonel.

"I can get along with that," answered Nick.

"But I want to ask you a few questions first. Why did you tell me that Wolf was working against me?"

"Because he was. He knew very well that you were after Waddie and the rest of them, and he sent me over to the Horse Shoe to tell them to clear out."

"Why did you tell Colonel Wimpleton that the party were together, and that they were on better terms than they ought to be?" I inquired.

"That's my business; but, as I shall not be seen again in these parts, I don't mind telling," said he, with a coarse grin. "Miss Minnie was rather fond of me, and —"

"You impudent rascal!" exclaimed the colonel.

"O, it was so! She told me so herself. I was a little mad because Tommy Toppleton was likely to cut me out."

"You may go now. I don't want to see or hear any more of you," replied Colonel Wimpleton, disgusted with the fellow's conceit.

"Where can I go now? I have lost the train," added Nick, as he glanced at the wagon.

"Go where you please; but don't let me see you in these parts again," replied the great man, as he stepped into the vehicle.

I took my seat at his side. The colonel opened the roll of bills which Nick had restored to him, and gave him the sum he had promised. I could not help thinking that it was a very handsome reward for a small service. When this business was done, I took the reins, and drove back to Hitaca. We arrived just in time for the colonel to take the railroad boat, which started at quarter of twelve. After dinner, I obtained some provisions for the Belle, and sailed for home. Unfortunately, the wind was light from the north, where it had been on my voyage up the lake, and from Port Gunga I was obliged to beat all the way down. It was nine o'clock when I arrived at Middleport, and I went directly home.

"What's going on, Wolf?" asked my father.

"Colonel Wimpleton and I have made it all up," I replied.

"I'm so glad!" exclaimed my mother.

"He told me I might take command of the Ucayga again; but I don't think I shall. How did Van Wolter make out going down to-day?"

"Lost the trains this morning; for he would not go through the Horse Shoe Channel. He just saved them this afternoon. There is a great deal of grumbling."

"I will go pilot in her to-morrow," I added.

"Why not captain?"

"I'm really sorry for Van Wolter. He is a good, honest man, and I don't like to displace him. I hope a new arrangement will be made soon."

My father was curious to know what had passed between the colonel and myself; but I told him I was not at liberty to inform him, and he was reasonable enough not to require me to violate the confidence of the magnate. I told him, however, that we were better friends than ever before, and, what I regarded as the best news of all, that Colonel Wimpleton had stopped drinking.

For some reason or other, I felt happier that night than for years before. I could not help believing that there was "a good time coming." Everything looked more hopeful to me than ever before. One thing was very surprising to me. In the long talk I had had with Colonel Wimpleton, he had not even alluded to the matter which had so excited his indignation on the day we went to Grass Springs. Not a word had he said about Tommy Toppleton and Miss Minnie, or about Waddie and Grace. I had expected him to speak of this subject, and I feared it; for, as I was not disposed to deceive him, it would have been a very embarrassing topic to me. I was almost prepared to believe that he intended to let the young people follow their own inclinations, if they had any inclinations of this kind.

At half past eight the next morning I was on the wharf when the Ucayga arrived from up the lake. I saw John, the colonel's man, hand Van Wolter a note, as I went on board. He opened it, and read its contents.

"I'm glad to see you, Wolf," said he, as I pre-

16

sented myself. "I am ordered to report to you as captain of the Ucayga again," said Van Wolter.

"I have not received my appointment as captain," I replied. "Of course I cannot take the command without authority."

"Here it is."

"That is not directed to me. I want you to keep your place, Van Wolter, for the present. I will be your pilot to-day; and, when I have seen Colonel Wimpleton, I hope it will be all right with both of us."

He objected, but I prevailed upon him at last to pocket the note, and retain his position. I took the Ucayga through the Horse Shoe Channel on that trip, and she was on time. When I returned at noon, Colonel Wimpleton came on board, and gave me a very pleasant greeting.

"What does Van Wolter say about his boy?" he asked.

"Not a word. Of course he does not know anything about the affair of yesterday."

"You can tell him that Nick has gone to California, if you believe he has gone there."

"I do not believe it. I think we had better say nothing about him. Probably he will come back when he has spent his money."

"Well, what does Van Wolter say about losing his place as captain?"

"I don't think he has lost it yet. I have not been appointed."

"I thought you would consider what I said yesterday as an appointment."

"Not exactly, sir," I replied. "I was in hopes that you would make me the agent of the line."

"I have thought about that matter, Wolf," he replied, struggling to conceal a frown. "We will consider it."

We took seats in my state-room for this purpose.

CHAPTER XXII.

SEVEN PER CENT. BONDS.

"WOLF, I have decided that I will have nothing to do with the consolidation of the two lines," said Colonel Wimpleton, as he seated himself in the state-room.

"I am sorry for that, sir," I replied, my heart sinking under the declaration, for I had permitted my hopes to run very high.

"I cannot do anything which looks like receding from my position."

"Though I am greatly disappointed, sir, of course I have no right to complain."

"You shall have no reason to complain. I purpose to leave the whole matter in the hands of the Steamboat Company," he added, with a smile on his face which seemed to be struggling with a frown for the mastery of his expression.

"To the students?" I inquired, unable to believe that I heard him right; for leaving the matter to the Steamboat Company was precisely the same thing as yielding the point.

"Yes, to the students," he answered, pursing up his lips, as though he were afraid I should see that what he was doing afforded him pleasure.

"Will you do me the favor to withdraw the order you sent to Captain Van Wolter?" I asked, delighted with the prospect, and almost giddy under the sudden change of the colonel.

"Certainly I will, if you desire it. Send for him."

I called Van Wolter from the wheel-house, and he gave up the note he had received.

"That means that you are still captain of the boat," said the colonel to Van Wolter.

"I was quite satisfied to give up the place, sir; for I want to say that I shall never dare to take the boat through the Horse Shoe Channel again," replied the captain.

"For the present I will act as your pilot," I interposed.

Van Wolter withdrew, and I was curious to know

whether the colonel intended to give the Steamboat Company definite instructions in regard to the consolidation of the two lines, or leave it to the members.

"Do you go up to Hitaca in the boat to-night, Wolf?"

"No, sir. I shall only act as pilot for the Horse Shoe Channel until the Steamboat Company makes its arrangement."

"Then I wish to see you in my library when you return from Ucayga. I have a little business to transact with you."

"I will be there, sir. But do you not intend to indicate your wishes in regard to the union or consolidation of the two lines?"

"I do not, though I would like to hear what the arrangement is before it is proposed to the other side."

"You shall be informed, sir."

He went on the wharf, and I saw him drive off in his buggy. I was never so happy in my life. The young peacemakers had a fine prospect of success, and I was very impatient to see Waddie, and inform him of what had taken place.

"What's going on, Captain Penniman?" asked Van Wolter, as I passed him on my way to the shore.

"There may be some change in the running of the boat," I replied.

"But who is to be captain of the Ucayga?"

"I don't know yet; but, as you have been faithful to me, I do not intend to desert you."

"Thank you, Wolf. You are a Christian," added he, with a grateful smile.

"I will go down the lake with you this afternoon," I continued, as I stepped upon the wharf.

I hastened to the Institute, and considered myself justified in asking to see Waddie before the session was closed; and we took a seat in the playground.

"What's the matter now, Wolf?" asked my friend, satisfied from my coming at such a time that I had something important to communicate.

"Nothing is the matter."

"You went up to Hitaca with my father night before last."

"I did; but that has nothing to do with my

present business," I replied, evasively. "Finding your father in pretty good humor, after what Major Toppleton had done, I opened the matter of uniting the two lines again."

"Good!" exclaimed Waddie. "By the great horn spoon, I wish it could be done."

"It can be."

"You don't mean so."

"I think it can; though your father will not have anything to do with it himself."

"How can it be done, then?"

"He says he will leave it to the Steamboat Company, and they may do as they think best."

"Then it is done!" shouted Waddie, jumping up, and capering about like a crazy man.

"Call a meeting at once."

"I'll do it."

"At the close of the session this forenoon?"

"Yes; but what shall we do?"

"Simply appoint a committee of three, with full powers to make any arrangement they think proper."

"Will you attend the meeting, Wolf?" asked Waddie, anxiously.

"No; I cannot. I have to pilot the boat down to Ucayga; but I will meet the committee, at half past six, wherever you say," I replied.

"All right. This is first rate, Wolf — isn't it?"

"Yes, it is; ever so much better than I expected. But I can stay no longer, for I have only time to go over and see Tommy, and get him to call a meeting of the Railroad Company."

"You are captain of the steamer again, Wolf," said Waddie, laughing.

"No; Van Wolter was displaced, though I was not appointed; but your father has recalled the order. I'm ambitious, Waddie, and I am looking for a better place than that of captain."

"What's that?"

"I want to be general agent of the two lines when they are united. I think I can do more good in that capacity than in any other."

"You shall have the place if you want it."

"I do," I replied, as I left him.

Crossing the lake, I found Tommy Toppleton at his studies. I stated the case to him, and he promised to call a meeting of the stockholders if his father consented. It did not occur to me that Major Toppleton would offer any opposition to the plan, and I returned to Centreport, satisfied that my hopes would soon be realized. After making the trip down the lake, I called upon Colonel Wimpleton, as I had agreed to do.

"Well, Wolf, what have you done about consolidation?" he asked, with a smile.

"Both companies were to call meetings, and by this time I suppose each has chosen a committee of conference."

"Very well; I don't intend to meddle with the matter. I wished to see you upon other business. Have you heard anything more from Nick Van Wolter?"

"No, sir; not a word."

"Doesn't his father say anything?"

"Of course not. Probably he thinks his son is in some hotel in Hitaca."

"But he would be likely to inquire about him, then, for he spends the night at the upper end of the lake.'

"He has not mentioned him to me. I don't think Nick will come back till his money is spent."

"We are well rid of him. I suppose, Wolf, that ten thousand dollars in cash would be rather embarrassing to you; and instead of it, I have made up the amount in good paying bonds, yielding seven per cent."

"Bonds?" I inquired, bewildered by his speech.

"If you prefer cash, you shall have it," added he.

"I don't prefer either. I don't understand what you mean."

"Didn't Nick rob you of your check?"

"I didn't regard it as my check. I burned mine."

"Come, Wolf, we will not be at loggerheads on this matter. When I gave you that check I *gave* it to you; and, if my pride would permit me to withhold the gift now, my sense of duty would not. You must take either the money or the bonds."

"I have no right to either, sir," I pleaded. "I don't know but so much money would spoil me."

"I think nothing will spoil you, Wolf."

"I will not deny that it would be very pleasant to me to have the money; but the manner of getting it does not suit me so well. If it is to purchase my silence —"

"Nonsense!" interrupted he, impatiently. "You have put more than double this amount into my pocket by your management of the steamer. You have saved my life, and saved me from shame and disgrace. I insist that you take it. Shall it be in cash or bonds?"

"In bonds, sir," I replied, yielding the point; and for the first time in my life I felt that I was a rich man.

He handed me a package containing the securities.

"I am all the richer, Wolf, for giving you this."

"I don't know, sir, but that it will bother me to conceal from my father and mother the reason for my having so much wealth."

"Tell your father and mother as much as you please, then; but don't let me be talked about in the streets, if you can help it."

"I will be very prudent, sir, and my father will also."

"When does the committee of the Steamboat Company meet, Wolf?"

"At half past six this afternoon."

"Will you tell Waddie I wish to see him before they meet?"

"Yes, sir."

"I do not intend to meddle with the business, only to make a suggestion to him."

I left him, with the securities in my pocket, hardly able to believe that I was Wolf Penniman. When I saw Waddie, I sent him to his father; but he appeared promptly at the place appointed for the meeting of the Steamboat committee. The members were Waddie, who had again been elected president, Ben Pinkerton, and Dick Bayard.

"I believe the world is coming to an end," said Ben, after he had cordially greeted me.

"No; only the war between the two sides of the lake," I replied.

"Well, Wolf, we are fully authorized to act for our Company," interposed Waddie, who was impatient to proceed with the business. "We can do anything we like with the Company, even if we sink it."

"You talk about consolidation and union," said Dick Bayard. "I don't think these words mean the same thing."

"I know they don't," I replied.

"Consolidation means union, but union don't mean consolidation," added Ben Pinkerton. "By the former, the two Companies would be fused into one; by the latter, they would only run their respective lines in connection with each other."

"I suppose we are to determine whether we unite or consolidate," said Waddie.

"I shall be satisfied with either," I replied.

The committee discussed the question for some time, and finally agreed to make a proposition to the Railroad Company, first, to consolidate, and then, if this plan failed, to unite. All the terms of both plans were settled, and this committee were prepared to meet the other.

"There is one more point," said Ben Pinkerton. "Whether we consolidate or unite, it is necessary to have a general agent, and I move that this committee, on its part, appoint Captain Wolf Penniman."

The motion was carried, after it had been seconded by Dick Bayard.

"I move that his salary, to be paid by the consolidated Company, or by both Companies, in the ratios of the fares, be fifteen hundred dollars a year," added Dick.

"I beg you will not mention this subject yet," I interposed. "It is rather premature."

"Not at all," replied Waddie. "This must be part of the bargain."

The motion was instantly carried; and I learned that this was the matter upon which the colonel had wished to see his son. The business was done, and I went home. The next evening the two committees met in conference.

CHAPTER XXIII.

THE COMMITTEE OF CONFERENCE.

THE committee of conference met at the railroad station in Middleport, and I was invited to be present on the interesting occasion. On the part of the Railroad Company, Tommy Toppleton, Ned Skotchley, and Bob Briscoe appeared. Each was ready to suggest a plan for a union of the two lines. Major Toppleton had assented to the union; but he insisted upon knowing the terms before final action was taken.

"I have a plan for consolidating the two Companies," said Waddie.

"What, making one Company of the two?" asked Tommy.

"Yes."

"I don't know about that. I don't see how it can be done."

"Very easily, I think," answered Waddie. "The capital stock of the Railroad Company is two hundred thousand; of the Steamboat Company one hundred thousand. We make a new corporation, with a capital of three hundred thousand, of which you own two thirds, and we one third."

"But the Steamboat Company has not a hundred thousand dollars' worth of property," suggested Tommy. "The Ucayga did not cost that."

"No, she did not; but the Company have really the monopoly of the through travel, and the line pays a dividend of twenty per cent. on a hundred thousand dollars. Our side does not gain anything by consolidation. The people of Centreport and Ruoara will not be so well accommodated under the new arrangement as they are now," responded Waddie.

"But you will have your share of the railroad profits," suggested Tommy.

"What were your dividends last year?" asked the President of the Steamboat Company, with a smile.

"They will be much larger under the new arrangement."

"And those of the steamer will be much smaller."

"We have spent fully two hundred thousand on the railroad," added Briscoe. "We have just laid down new rails, and built a bridge over the river at the foot of the lake."

"And we have two steamers," added Skotchley.

"Let the steamers be sold, if they are not wanted," said Ben Pinkerton.

"And let the purchaser set up an opposition line," replied Tommy.

"But Middleport would have two votes in a stockholders' meeting to one from Centreport."

"No; one of the conditions is, that the stock may be equalized by the payment of its par value, at the option of the Steamboat Company."

Each party felt it necessary to be very sharp, and every point and proposition was disputed, for the holders of the mortgage bonds of each company — Colonel Wimpleton and Major Toppleton — were to revise and approve their action. At nine o'clock in the evening no progress had been made, and I was satisfied that there were too many obstacles in the way of consolidation. I thought it very doubtful whether the colonel would allow his property in the steamer to pass into the control of the other side. I suggested, therefore, that the other and more simple method be considered.

"Let each company run its own line on its own hook," said Waddie. "We will convey the passengers from Hitaca to Middleport, and you to Ucayga. Each party is to have the exclusive right to his own share of the line."

"But that leaves two steamers on our hands for which we shall then have no use," objected Tommy.

"They are not worth much," laughed Ben Pinkerton.

"They are worth too much to be permitted to rot at the wharf," answered Tommy. "We don't want steamers if we are to have no use for them."

"That's so," added Briscoe. "It is fair for the Steamboat Company to buy our boats."

"What do you think, Wolf?"

"I am not one of the high contracting powers, and perhaps I ought not to say anything," I replied, lightly.

"Don't stand on any ceremony, Wolf."

"Well, then, I think Briscoe's suggestion is a fair one."

"What do you ask for them?" inquired Waddie.

"They ought to be appraised by three disinterested men," I added. "Both parties should be bound to their award."

"I think we ought to have what they cost," said Tommy. "We paid the par value of the shares for the stock we bought."

"I don't think so," interposed Dick Bayard, catching the point. "They are not worth so much now, when there is no use for them."

This point was discussed at considerable length; but my proposition was finally adopted.

"Now, how shall the fares be divided?" said Tommy.

"In the ratio of the distance which each line carries the passengers," replied Pinkerton.

"That's not fair," added Briscoe. "It costs more to run a railroad than a steamboat. The ratio of the time ought to be taken into the account."

"I don't see it," interposed Waddie.

"If we shorten the time half or three quarters of

an hour by uniting the two lines, the Steamboat Company has the benefit of it, though it is the railroad that does it," argued Briscoe. "The Ucayga's best time now is three hours and a half. If I understand Captain Penniman, under the new arrangement the time is to be three hours from Hitaca to Ucayga."

"Exactly so," I answered.

"Then it is the railroad that shortens the time, and the Steamboat Company has the benefit of it," continued Briscoe, triumphantly. "I move you the division be equal. We take the Steamboat Company's checks, and they take ours. In settlement each party shall pay the other one dollar to redeem its own checks."

The committee on the part of the steamer yielded this point, after some further discussion.

"Now we want a general agent for both lines," said Waddie.

"With your permission I will retire while this subject is considered," I interposed; and, without waiting for a reply, I went out of the room.

I had not been absent five minutes before I was

recalled, and informed that I was to be recommended as the general agent, at a salary of fifteen hundred a year, half of which was to be paid by each Company. I returned my thanks for the honor done me, and for the liberality of the salary. Many other details of the proposed union were settled, and it was eleven o'clock before the business was finished. I went with Tommy to his father's house, and the major carefully read the agreement, as it had been drawn up by the secretary of the railroad committee. Somewhat to my surprise, he took a pen and wrote his approval upon it.

"It's a fair thing," said he. "You have done the business well, Tommy. I am afraid Wimpleton will not agree to it."

"Why not, father?" asked Tommy, anxiously.

"Because there are two things in the agreement which may not seem to be fair on the face of them — the purchase of our two steamers, and the equal division of the fares;" and the major went over about the same arguments that had been used in the committee of conference.

I confess that I went to bed that night not a little worried at the fate of the plan on the other side of the lake. In the morning I went over to take my place on board of the Ucayga. I found Waddie there, and with rather a long face.

"What does your father say?" I asked, though Waddie's face had already answered the question.

"He said he would not have anything to do with the matter."

"Will he indorse the agreement?"

"He will give his formal assent to everything we have done, but nothing more."

"That's all we want."

"Not quite. He will not purchase the two old steamers," added Waddie. "He says they are old tubs, of no use now, and he is not disposed to take them off the major's hands. Perhaps you can move him, Wolf. Nobody else can."

Waddie was despondent. He had objected to purchasing the steamers, and had only yielded after consulting me. I was confident that the colonel could be brought over.

"If your father will agree to all the rest, Waddie, I will see that the purchase of the steamers does not break up the arrangement," I replied.

"What can you do?"

"O, I will buy them myself, and set up an opposition line," I answered, laughing.

"You are the general agent, Wolf."

"I can resign."

"But you would not do that, even if you could buy the steamers."

"Probably not; but here comes your father. I will talk about the matter with him."

Colonel Wimpleton came on board. He looked very good-natured.

"I am going down to Ucayga, Wolf."

"I am glad of it, for I wish to speak with you," I replied.

"Do you wish to convince me that I ought to throw half our business into the hands of Toppleton, and then compensate myself for the loss by buying those old boats, which are not worth five thousand dollars apiece, though they cost him double that sum?"

"I don't wish to convince you against your judgment, sir."

"I can't buy them. If the Steamboat Company

can make an arrangement to run in connection with the railroad, I will offer no objection; but when they ask me to buy two old tubs — that's quite another thing."

"Do you think the two boats are worth ten thousand dollars?" I asked.

"Just about that."

"Then I will buy them, sir," I replied, as modestly as I could in uttering so grand a proposition.

"You, Wolf!"

"I mean so, sir."

"What for?" he asked, opening his eyes in amazement.

"I think I could get more than seven per cent. for my money out of them."

"If you can, then I can."

"I might set up an opposition line with them," I replied, laughing.

"An opposition line!"

"Or, if I had not the conscience to do it myself, some one else might. In a word, sir, if you are going to run the Ucayga from Hitaca to Middleport, you ought to control all the passenger steamers on the lake."

"That's true, Wolf."

"If Major Toppleton keeps those boats, he has a hold upon you which you may feel when any misunderstanding occurs."

"Just so."

"Besides, you want those boats, sir. If you can buy them cheap, it will pay to run them as ferry boats — one between Centreport and Middleport, and the other between Ruoara and Spangleport."

"Well, Wolf, I don't care about bothering with referees. You may offer Toppleton ten thousand dollars for the two," continued the colonel, who, I was satisfied, did not really object to the terms of the union, but, rather from the force of habit than for any other reason, deemed it necessary to offer some resistance to his old enemy.

I had not expected this easy victory in the argument, and I was convinced that Colonel Wimpleton was an altered man. I doubt whether he had seen a time in three years before when he was entirely free from liquor. He had always been a regular drinker, and for several years an immoderate one. I was forced to attribute his former malignity to the rum in which he had steeped himself.

The colonel went down to Ucayga in the steamer, and went on shore. As he did so I saw the landlord of the hotel at Grass Springs step up to him, and, with an exceedingly supercilious air, present him a paper. I was interested at once, and, while the boat lay at the wharf, I observed them very closely. The colonel appeared to be considerably excited, and looked at the paper the landlord had given him with great apparent interest. As the bell rang for the steamer to start, he came on board, followed by his companion.

CHAPTER XXIV.

THE MAGNATES JOIN HANDS.

JUST as the deck hands were hauling in the plank, Major Toppleton rushed down and leaped on deck. Probably he was not aware of the fact that Colonel Wimpleton was on board, or he would not have incurred the liability of seeing him. I concluded that he was nervous about the arrangements for the union of the two lines, and wished to see me in relation to them.

I had nothing to do till the steamer reached the North Shoe, and I sat down near the door of my state-room. Presently Colonel Wimpleton appeared on the hurricane deck, closely followed by the landlord of the hotel.

"Wolf, this little bill has just been handed to me," said the magnate of Centreport, giving me the paper.

"What is it, sir?"

"Read it for yourself."

"Captain Penniman will see that it is all right," added the landlord, whose name was Sharp.

I glanced at the bill. It was so absurd that I could not help laughing. The charges were all for damage done to his house and furniture by the colonel, during his visit to the hotel. The items were as follows: —

To damage done to bed and bedding,	$400
" spilling ink, and spoiling carpet, .	300
" damage to bureau and chairs, . .	200
" keeping still about it, ...	300
	$1200

"What do you mean by this, Mr. Sharp?" I inquired.

"I mean just what it says in that bill," he replied, with a brazen face.

"Do you expect me to pay that bill?" demanded the colonel, indignantly.

"I will leave that to you, sir; but I think you will pay it, as much for your own sake as mine."

"This is the most impudent piece of extortion I ever saw attempted," added the magnate.

"Well, sir, if people will dance they must pay the fiddler."

"Why, all the furniture in the room was not worth a hundred dollars," said the indignant colonel.

"I don't want to say much about the matter, Colonel Wimpleton. If you are not willing to pay the bill, I don't care about arguing the matter. If you don't pay it up, it won't be my fault if people don't know what took place in that room."

The great man turned pale. The consequences of his debauch followed him in such humiliating demands as this bill.

"Why didn't you put it all down under the last item of 'keeping still about it'?" added Colonel Wimpleton; but he was alarmed at the threat of the landlord, and his speech was very mild.

"It is an outrageous imposition," I ventured to say, when I found it quite impossible to keep still.

"That comes very well from you, Captain Penniman, after you have had your nest feathered," sneered Sharp.

In my turn, I was abashed at this home thrust, though I could not believe that it was anything more than a supposition on his part.

"I never attempted to extort money from any person," I replied. "I was with Colonel Wimpleton, and I say this bill is a swindle. I hope he will not think of such a thing as paying even a penny of it."

"He can do as he thinks best," the fellow doggedly replied.

"There isn't a shadow of justice in it," I added, as the colonel stepped into the state-room, and seated himself there, evidently to prevent any one from seeing him.

"He was the drunkest man that ever came into my house," continued Sharp; "and, if he wants to keep it out of the newspapers, he had better pay up."

"What's the matter, Sharp?" said Major Toppleton, approaching the spot at this moment.

"Ah, I didn't know you were here, sir!" exclaimed the landlord, with a start.

The major stopped before he came in front of the state-room door, and he did not see that his old rival was within. With the bill in my hand, — for I had not yet given it back to the colonel, — I beckoned the magnate of Middleport away from the dangerous locality.

"What's the matter, Wolf?" asked he, mystified by my movement.

"Colonel Wimpleton is in that state-room," I replied, when we had walked abaft the engine.

"Whew!" whistled he. "I did not know he was on board; but I wanted to see you about this union of the two lines."

"He did not see you, sir; and Sharp has moved away from the door, so he will not tell him you are here."

"I don't care about meeting him just now," laughed the major.

"I thought you would not, and so I beckoned you away. You know Sharp, the landlord?"

I knew he did, for I was aware that the major owned the hotel in Grass Springs, and had set Sharp up in his business.

"I know he is not the man I took him to be when I assisted him to his present position," replied the major. "He seems to be excited about something."

"Read this bill," I added, handing him the document.

Major Toppleton opened his eyes as he examined the account.

"Is this a joke?" he asked.

"No, sir; Sharp actually demands twelve hundred dollars of Colonel Wimpleton. The last item is hush-money, but it all comes under that head."

"The miserable scoundrel!" exclaimed the major, indignantly. "I am tempted to kick him."

"He says the colonel was the drunkest man that ever entered his house, and, if he does not pay this swindle, everybody shall know it."

"What if he was drunk? The man that sells him the liquor is not the one to condemn and expose him. I will give the scoundrel a lesson he will never forget. Sharp!" said he, as the landlord, who was pacing the deck rather nervously, passed within hailing distance of him.

"At your service, Major Toppleton," replied Sharp, in cringing tones.

"What have you been doing? What does this bill mean?"

The wretch started when he saw the account in the hands of his powerful patron. Knowing the enmity which had so long existed between the two sides of the lake, and especially between the two great men, he would have counted upon the assistance rather than the opposition of Major Toppleton in any movement against his rival.

"Colonel Wimpleton came to my house the drunkest man I ever saw," replied he.

"And you are going to swindle him for it!" added the major, severely. "Sharp, your lease expires in July; it will not be renewed. I will not tolerate such a scoundrel."

"If you don't think it is right — "

"Right! you villain! Is it ever right to swindle a man?"

"But it was Colonel Wimpleton, and — "

"No matter who it was. Colonel Wimpleton is a gentleman, and if he were a hundred times my enemy, I would stand up for him against any such miserable trick as this."

"I won't say anything more about it, Major Toppleton," pleaded Sharp.

"But I will. I will go to every man within ten miles of Grass Springs, and tell him you are a liar, a swindler, and a scoundrel," continued the major, much excited, as he shook his fist in the face of the

THE MAGNATES JOIN HANDS. Page 275.

landlord. "In this matter Colonel Wimpleton is my best friend."

"Major Toppleton!"

To my surprise, Colonel Wimpleton stepped out from behind the engine, and walking square up to his old enemy, extended his hand to him.

"I was not aware that you were near," said the major, rather startled.

"I offer you my hand, Major Toppleton," said the colonel, his lip quivering with emotion.

"I accept it," replied the magnate of Middleport.

They grasped hands. If there had been any artillery on board the Ucayga, I should have fired a hundred guns in honor of this auspicious event. As it was, I called Van Wolter, and asked him to display every piece of bunting on the steamer. I was so delighted that it seemed to me I should "go up." The young peacemakers had been at work for a year to bring about this result; but both of the great men had hung back. I did not consider that the reconciliation was actually made on the deck of the Ucayga. The major had been prepared for it for months, and the colonel from the time the steamer was hauled off the sands by the Ruoara. Neither had had the courage to approach the other, and I regarded the coming of the landlord as a fortunate event.

Sharp hung his head with shame, as he saw the magnates join hands. He had brought his bill to a bad market. I wondered whether Nick Van Wolter had not put him up to this trick. The fellow had boldly told me that my nest had been feathered, and no one but Nick had known about the check until it was drawn.

"Major Toppleton, probably you understand this matter now," said the colonel, still trembling with emotion.

"I know nothing about it, except that this scoundrel was trying to swindle you. I have already told him his lease would not be renewed," replied the major, still holding the hand of his old rival. "Whatever differences we have had, I know you to be a gentleman and a man of honor; and I would protect even an enemy from such a swindle as this."

"I trust we shall no longer be enemies," added Colonel Wimpleton.

"Not by my choice, certainly," answered the major.

"Our boys and girls have set us a good example. They have made peace among themselves, and we ought not to be behind them in this matter."

I was obliged to go to the wheel, as the steamer was approaching the North Shoe; but I was so excited by the auspicious event which had just transpired, that I was afraid I should run the boat aground myself, as Van Wolter had done. But I had hardly taken my place at the wheel before both the major and the colonel entered, and continued their conversation. The unwonted sight of the two great men talking together on friendly terms had been noticed by the passengers, and they were gathering on the hurricane deck to witness the strange exhibition. The two gentlemen were annoyed by the interest manifested in their affairs, and retreated to the wheel-house to escape observation.

"I must beg you to retire to the captain's state-room, gentlemen," I interposed. "I am so interested in what you say, that I am afraid I shall run the steamer aground if I listen to it."

I pointed to the door which opened from the wheel-house into the state-room, and they were considerate enough to retire.

"The world's coming to an end," said Van Wolter, standing opposite me at the wheel.

"On the contrary, I think it is only just beginning to exist," I replied; and it did seem to me that we were all about to enter upon a new life — a life of peace.

"They have really made up."

"They have indeed. I wish we had a twenty-four pounder on board," I continued. "I would make a noise in honor of the event."

"I have put out all the bunting we have, and it makes quite a show."

"Everything will go right now, and the union will certainly be arranged," I added.

"What union?" asked Van Wolter, who had had no hint of the negotiations in progress.

"The union of the two lines. In a short time, this boat will make two trips a day from Middleport to Hitaca, connecting with the railroad."

"You don't say it!" exclaimed Van Wolter.

"The two companies split on only one point. That will be arranged now."

"I suppose one of the captains of the old boats will take this one, then," added he, rather gloomily.

"Not at all. I am to be general agent for both lines, and you will remain in command of this boat."

"Is that so?"

"I shall insist upon this arrangement. I never go back on a good friend."

"You are a Christian, Captain Penniman."

"I try to be one. You will have no more trouble about the Horse Shoe Channel. You must make yourself agreeable to your passengers, and I have no doubt you will be as popular as you deserve to be."

As we approached the bend of the channel the conversation was discontinued; but, when I could leave the helm, I joined the magnates in the stateroom.

CHAPTER XXV.

MORE SEVEN PER CENT. BONDS.

WHEN I entered the state-room where the magnates were, Colonel Wimpleton was inviting Major Toppleton to dine with him that day. Men are apt to go from one extreme to the other, and, from the exceeding cordiality of the reunion, I was afraid they might overdo the matter. Yet they had once been warm personal friends, and had chosen this locality on the lake in order to be near each other. Long and bitter had the quarrel been; but now, by the influence of the young peacemakers, it was happily ended.

"Wolf, you must dine with us," said Colonel Wimpleton, as I entered the state-room. "We will smoke the pipe of peace to-day."

"I thank you; I never smoke, but I will dine with you," I replied. "At what hour?"

"Three o'clock."

"Then I shall be obliged to decline, for I must pilot the boat down this afternoon."

"We will make it six o'clock, then. Major Toppleton, you must bring all your family with you."

"They will all be very happy to come," answered the magnate of Middleport.

Then Grace would be there, which offered an additional inducement to me. I concluded that the colonel would not say anything more about "courting," though I happened to know that Tommy and Miss Minnie had met two or three times since the affair off the Horse Shoe.

"You will excuse me, gentlemen, for speaking of business at such a time as this; but I should like to know if you have agreed upon the terms of the union between the two lines," I continued.

"We have not mentioned the subject," said Major Toppleton. "Whatever Colonel Wimpleton agrees to, I shall fully indorse."

"I am authorized to make you an offer for the two steamers, Major Toppleton," I added.

"You needn't make the offer, Wolf," interposed

the colonel. "I will accept the terms of the arrangement in all respects, as drawn up by the committee of conference."

"If the arrangement is not entirely satisfactory, I will modify it in any manner my friend Colonel Wimpleton may suggest."

"Everything is entirely satisfactory to me," persisted he of Centreport.

"But you did raise an objection," insisted he of Middleport.

"Colonel Wimpleton thought it was not worth while to bother with referees to fix the value of the two steamers," I interposed. "Of course nothing can be done till they have been appraised."

"That's an excellent suggestion of my friend. What was the offer, Wolf?" asked the major.

"Don't mention it, Wolf," said the colonel.

"I accept it, whatever it was," continued the major.

"We had not met when I authorized Wolf to make the offer. I am ashamed of it now," added the colonel.

"I think I can settle this matter, gentlemen, to

the satisfaction of both of you," I ventured to say. "You shall each mark the price on a piece of paper, and the sum to be paid shall be found by splitting the difference between the two."

"I agree," said Major Toppleton, promptly.

"So do I," as promptly replied Colonel Wimpleton.

I gave each of them a piece of paper and a pencil.

"I shall take into consideration the fact that the new arrangement renders the old boats of less value than they are in the railroad line," said the major, as he wrote his valuation on the paper, and handed it to me.

Colonel Wimpleton made his figures, and gave me his paper. One was eight thousand, — the major's, — the other twelve thousand. Half the difference between them, added to the smaller, or taken from the greater, gave the agreed price.

"Just the amount I was authorized to offer," said I, exhibiting the two papers.

"I am satisfied," replied the colonel.

"So am I," added the major.

"The question is settled, then," I continued.

"Wolf, where is Sharp?" asked the major.

"Probably he went on shore at Ruoara," I replied.

"I will clean him out on the first of next month."

"Not on my account," interposed the colonel.

"I will not permit so great a scoundrel as he is to occupy a house of mine," protested the major.

"His tongue may cause me some annoyance," added the colonel, fixing his gaze upon the floor.

"You may be sure that he will never utter a word to your disparagement."

"I am aware that I have given him cause to—"

"My dear colonel, we are all human," interrupted Major Toppleton. "But, if Sharp says a word against you, I shall consider it as said against myself. Give yourself no uneasiness about it. I will take care of him."

"You are very kind and considerate, major. I wish to tell you what I told Wolf the other night— that I have determined never to taste intoxicating drinks in any form again. If there is no wine on my table to-day,—and there will not be,—you will understand the reason. It was absolutely necessary for me to 'brake up.'"

Major Toppleton politely changed the topic, which

was even more embarrassing to him than to the colonel. The Ucayga was approaching the wharf at Centreport, and the two gentlemen came out of the state-room.

"Why do you show so much bunting to-day, Wolf?" asked Colonel Wimpleton, when, for the first time, he discovered the display of flags.

"In honor of the great event of the day," I replied.

"It is a great event — isn't it?" he added, with a smile.

"The greatest thing that ever happened, sir!"

The boat was made fast to the wharf, and, as the major wished to return home at once, the colonel directed Captain Van Wolter to run the Ucayga over to the Middleport side, and went over himself. For my own part, I went on shore, for I was in a hurry to see Waddie, and give him the astounding news. I hastened up to the Institute, and called him out.

"What's up, Wolf?" asked he, anxiously, as he met me in the principal's office. "I hope nothing has gone wrong with the union."

"No; that's all settled as square as a brick; but the biggest thing that ever occurred on the Western

Continent, since the landing of Columbus, took place to-day," I continued in high excitement.

"What's that, Wolf?"

"What do you guess, Waddie?"

"I can't guess. Why don't you tell me?"

"Your father and Major Toppleton shook hands to-day, and the war is ended."

"No! You don't mean so!" exclaimed Waddie, his eyes opening at the news.

"It's a fact."

"By the great horn spoon!"

"O, it's so! Do you see the Ucayga there, making a landing at Middleport?" I asked, pointing out the window.

"I see her."

"Your father sent her over to land the major, and he has gone with him himself."

"It's too good news to be true."

I sat down and told him all about it — how they happened to be on board of the Ucayga, and how Sharp had brought about the reconciliation. I was careful, however, not to expose the colonel's secret to his son, and there was something wanting to complete the narrative, which troubled Waddie.

"Wolf, there is something about that visit to Grass Springs which I don't understand," said he. "Tell me honestly; was not my father — wasn't he — "

Waddie blushed, and hung his head.

"I know what you mean, Waddie," I interposed. "It is all right now. Your father has not drank a drop since, and he never will again. Everything has turned out for the best, and we won't say a word about what is past and gone. Your father has invited Major Toppleton and all his family to dine with him at six o'clock to-day."

"By the great horn spoon, we must turn out the regiment this afternoon, and escort the major up to the house," said Waddie. "Where is Tommy Toppleton?"

"At home, I suppose."

"I must see him. Our battalion shall turn out, at any rate. We'll have a time over this."

Waddie was as enthusiastic as I supposed he would be. I left him, and went on board of the Ucayga on her arrival from the other side. I worked for an hour on the programme for the new line, which had now become a fixed fact, and then went over to Middleport to dinner. My father was at home, and the good news had preceded me, though I had to answer a great many questions.

"When does the new arrangement go into effect, Wolf?" asked my father.

"Next Monday, I think, if we can get the bills out in season."

"The Ucayga will not go down the lake then."

"No, sir. She will make two trips each way between Hitaca and Middleport."

"We shall have to hurry up, I suppose."

"No, not much. The boat will have to land at Hitaca, and return without any delay. At this end of the route she will wait two hours between trips."

"Do you mean to leave me in Hitaca over night?"

"No, sir; Christy will run the boat down in the morning, and return in her at night; you will leave Middleport at eleven, and be back again at three. You will be on duty from ten till four."

"That will not make a very hard day's work," laughed my father. "What are you going to do, Wolf? Van Wolter is to command the boat."

"I am to go and come, and draw my salary of fifteen hundred a year."

"Fifteen hundred!" exclaimed my father.

"Fifteen hundred dollars, Wolf!" repeated my mother.

"My total income will be about twenty-two hundred dollars a year," I added, as seriously as I could speak.

"Where is the rest of it to come from?" asked my father.

"From the income of my property."

"What property?"

"I declare I believe I have forgotten to mention that I am worth ten thousand dollars, besides what I have saved up from my salary. But it is true. I have the amount in bonds, which pay seven per cent."

"You don't mean so, Wolf," said my father.

"I would show them to you, but I deposited them in the vault of the Centreport bank for safe keeping."

"Where did you get so much money, Wolf?"

As Colonel Wimpleton allowed me to inform my parents, I told them the whole story about the check, and our trip to Hitaca.

"Well, Wolf, you are a richer man than I am; but I suppose you will help me out when I am short."

"O, certainly! Can I do anything for you now?"

"No; I'm doing very well myself, Wolf. This place is paid for, and I have something laid up for a rainy day."

"There's somebody at the front door," said my mother, as the door bell rang.

To my surprise Major Toppleton followed my sister, who had opened the door, into the kitchen, where we were at dinner.

"Wolf, here is a package for you," said the magnate, dropping it on the table, as I was rising to show him proper respect.

"What is it, sir?" I inquired, picking up the parcel, which had a marvellous resemblance to the one the other magnate had presented to me.

"It contains ten thousand dollars in seven per cent. bonds."

"Really, sir, I don't—"

"Yes, you do," laughed the major. "You are in a hurry; so am I, and we will make a short story of it. My friend Colonel Wimpleton"—the major's eyes twinkled—"told me what he had done for you in this way. My conscience would not let me do less than he has done. I am determined to be even with him. Good morning, Wolf!"

He turned on his heel, and fled from the house as though an enemy were after him. My father laughed, my mother cried, and I endeavored to keep cool. But it was time to return to the steamer, and we hastened to our duties.

CHAPTER XXVI.

IN HONOR OF THE RECONCILIATION.

THERE was evidently a conspiracy to make a rich man of me; and, if there had been any more magnates in the vicinity, I should certainly have expected a contribution from all of them. Vast as were the sums bestowed upon me, a poor boy, these were really but drops in the bucket to the *millionnaires* who gave them. I could find no excuse for the liberality of Major Toppleton, but I concluded not to quarrel with my destiny. The magnate of Middleport was certainly in condition to do business when he made the gift, and I was not willing to hurt his feelings by declining the princely present.

On the trip down to Ucayga I completed the programme for the new line. The trip from one end of the lake to the other was to be run in less than three hours, with time enough to spare to make up for a ten minutes' detention in both steamer and the railroad. The Ucayga was to leave Hitaca at seven in the morning, which was quite a reasonable hour. Connecting with the train at Middleport at nine, passengers were to reach Ucayga in ample time for the trains. On the return of the cars at eleven, the boat was to leave Middleport for Hitaca, and come back immediately, leaving Middleport for the last trip up the lake at five, and arriving at seven. The ferries were to convey passengers across the lake from Ruoara and Centreport. I was abundantly pleased with the programme, and was sure it would give satisfaction to all parties.

On the arrival of the boat at Ucayga, I was rather surprised to see a couple of brass field-pieces on the wharf, ready to be rolled on board. The appearance of Tommy Toppleton explained the meaning of them, though they were to be allowed to speak for themselves in the course of the day. Tommy, who was in full uniform as the colonel of the regiment, came up to me, on the hurricane deck. He was as lively and cheerful as the occasion required. He had seen Waddie, and the regiment was to form at Centreport in season for the festivities. He had procured the services of a detachment of the Ucayga Artillery to fire the salutes, which Waddie had suggested.

"We are going to make a big time of it," said Tommy, with enthusiasm. "We have engaged the band here, besides the one that belongs to the regiment — There they come. Waddie is going to have a grand collation in the grove near his father's house. If we don't wake things up, it will be because we haven't spunk enough to do it."

"It's a big thing, Tommy," I mildly suggested.

"That's so, Wolf; and more than anybody else, you have brought it about."

"Well, we have all been peacemakers," I modestly added.

"I never expected to see the day when my father and Colonel Wimpleton would shake hands and dine together. We will let off a hundred guns at six o'clock, when the two families sit down to supper," added Tommy. "By the way, Wolf, this is a splendid thing for me."

"It is for all of us."

"Well, I mean for me in particular," replied he, significantly.

"Why?"

"You needn't try to be dull, Wolf. Wasn't Colonel Wimpleton after me with a sharp stick the day we went down to Grass Springs?"

"O, you mean Miss Minnie?"

"To be sure I do — you are not stupid. I think Minnie is the prettiest girl in the state, and if I ever marry anybody, she will be my wife — that is, if she consents;" and Tommy's under jaw dropped a little, as though he realized that he had been talking too fast.

I told him I would guarantee her consent for one and a half per cent. of two and sixpence, whereat his face livened up again. I asked him into the stateroom to examine the programme of the new line. He indorsed it on the part of the Railroad Company.

As the boat approached Centreport we saw that there was an unusual stir on the wharf. The battalion from Middleport was landing, and the other was drawn up on the shore. Tommy prinked up his uniform, threw back his shoulders, and looked as soldierly as possible. His sorrel pony stood waiting for him, and Waddie was already mounted. As soon as the steamer touched the wharf I left her, and hastened to see the preparations for the great occasion.

"You are to ride in the barouche with the Toppletons, Wolf," said Waddie, dashing his fiery steed up to me as soon as I appeared, so furious that I trembled for my corns, for these military people are always very impressive.

"Thank you, Waddie. I suppose I could walk, on a pinch."

"No pinch about it; you must be escorted up to the house with our guests."

"All right; I surrender," I replied; when a toot from a trumpet startled his horse, and again imperilled my corns.

Tom Walton was sailing the Toppletons over in the Belle, which had nearly reached the shore. I was not posted in regard to the order of exercises, and I watched the proceedings with interest. The regiment was drawn up in line, with the band at the head. Colonel Wimpleton's barouche was at the end of the wharf, ready to receive the honored guests. The field officers were all mounted, and they kept flashing up and down the line, just as though something would burst if they did not make haste, and look especially savage. They could not have been more impressive if they had been engaged in a great battle upon which the fate of the nation depended.

As the Belle drew near the landing stairs, I hastened to greet the Toppletons. I had never seen Grace look prettier or more interesting, and the smile she bestowed upon me was a rapture to me. I assisted her out of the boat and up the steps to the carriage. Mrs. Toppleton and Grace occupied the back seat, while the major and myself sat on the front seat. Adjutant Briscoe mounted the box, to see that the driver complied with all the military forms.

"Present — arms!" shouted Colonel Tommy Toppleton, as the carriage started.

The major and I uncovered, while the ladies waved

their handkerchiefs. The band played "Hail to the Chief," though who the particular chief was I had no means of knowing. We passed the line, and the adjutant in charge of our party directed the driver to draw up at the side of the road. Half the regiment then marched by us, and a guard of honor, composed of twelve sergeants, was stationed on each side of the barouche.

"Forward — march!" shouted Colonel Tommy Toppleton.

"Drive on," added Briscoe; and the procession moved off.

Somewhat to the annoyance, perhaps, of the major and his lady, the line of march was through the principal streets of Centreport, and of course the sensation was tremendous. But, as the young peacemakers desired to make this display, no objection was offered by the guests, and in the carriage we voted that we were first-class lions. The procession entered the grounds of Colonel Wimpleton, and when the carriage stopped at the door of the mansion, the magnate and his lady appeared to welcome their guests. It was the first time the wives of the two magnates had met for many years; and, as they had not shared in the enmity of their husbands, the occasion was a joyful one to them. We were ushered into the drawing-room, and as the clock struck six, dinner was announced. At this moment, Colonel Tommy Toppleton and Lieutenant Colonel Waddie Wimpleton entered the room.

"Bang! bang!" spoke the guns which had been stationed in the grove, with a concussion that shook the windows of the house, and was rather trying to the nerves of the ladies.

At the same time the Ucayga band struck up "Met again," a familiar Sunday school air, known to everybody in that vicinity. Colonel Wimpleton gave his arm to Mrs. Toppleton, and Major Toppleton escorted Mrs. Wimpleton to the dinner table. Tommy took Miss Minnie, and I offered my arm to Miss Grace. Waddie, who seemed to be out in the cold, conducted one of his younger sisters, while the clergyman who had been invited led the other. When the party were seated, the minister said grace, in which he briefly alluded to the reconciliation, while the booming guns and the melodious strains still celebrated the happy event.

The dinner was a splendid affair, and, for one, I did full justice to it, for I have a weakness for good dinners, especially when they are given in honor of great events. The conversation soon became general, and the best feeling in the world prevailed. We talked of the events of the past, as well as of the present, and the reconciliation was perfect. I need not attempt to tell how much I enjoyed the society of Grace, who sat at my side.

After dinner, the party walked out into the grove, where the gallant soldiers of the regiment were banqueting in honor of the occasion. Grace leaned on my arm, and we had a delightful chat. When she called me Mr. Wolf, I asked her to omit the "Mr.," which she was kind enough to do.

"I suppose you know, Wolf, that you have done more than any one else to bring about this happy event," said she.

"I know that I have had it in my mind for several years. Your father wanted to continue the railroad to Hitaca, or build a new steamer; but I always advised him to do neither. I have tried to prevent quarrels; but, Grace, I think you have been the inspiration, in part at least, of my conduct. If you only approve it, I am happy."

"I do approve it, with all my heart," she replied, blushing.

I had not the courage to utter all that I felt, but I was sure that she had a very kind regard for me.

At eight o'clock the regiment again formed in line, and we were escorted down to the wharf, where we embarked in the Belle for Centreport. Major Toppleton had invited the Wimpletons to dine with him the next day, and the invitation had been accepted. I was not neglected.

With this happy occasion my story ought to close. The peace which was made that day was a lasting one, though, as is always the case even among the dearest friends, it was sometimes necessary for them to "BEAR AND FORBEAR." The two families dined together, the next day, at the major's, and the same programme was repeated, even to the parade of the regiment, the music, and the guns, that the Middleporters might make no possible mistake in regard to the reconciliation.

Handbills, announcing the new arrangement of the.

"Union Line," as I called it, were immediately issued, and on the following Monday all the Wimpletons and all the Toppletons went over the new route. We went Through by Daylight; the Lightning Express was On Time, and we did not find it necessary to Switch Off or Brake Up, in the moral sense, though both were done on the Lake Shore Railroad. The travelling public were pleased with the new arrangement, and even those who had to cross the lake in the ferries did not growl, for they were amply compensated for the extra trouble by the better time.

We heard nothing more of Nick Van Wolter for two months, though he turned up at the end of that time. I had a long talk with his father about him, and he acknowledged to me that the young man's mother was too ambitious in regard to him. Certainly her husband had proved to her that a faithful discharge of his duty in his own humble sphere was the safer course.

Colonel Wimpleton was true to his noble resolution. He drank no more; and the change in his morals was as great as in his manners. While his nature was the same, it was not depraved by intemperance, and he was a different man, though he was not always gentle and courteous.

When you find yourself indulging as he did in a bad habit, when you find your course of life is wrong in any respect, do as he did — "BRAKE UP."

www.ingramcontent.com/pod-product-compliance
Lightning Source LLC
Chambersburg PA
CBHW030809230426
43667CB00008B/1139